White Birch, Red Hawthorn

White Birch, Red Hawthorn

A Memoir

NORA MURPHY

University of Minnesota Press

Minneapolis | London

The University of Minnesota Press gratefully acknowledges the generous assistance provided for the publication of this book by the Margaret S. Harding Memorial Endowment, honoring the first director of the University of Minnesota Press.

Photograph: Rebecca S. Dallinger, *Mother Maple*, White Earth Reservation, 2016.

Published by the University of Minnesota Press
111 Third Avenue South, Suite 290
Minneapolis, MN 55401-2520
http://www.upress.umn.edu

ISBN 978-1-5179-0132-5 (pb)
A Cataloging-in-Publication record for this book is available from the Library of Congress.

Printed in the United States of America on acid-free paper

The University of Minnesota is an equal-opportunity educator and employer.

22 21 20 19 18 17   10 9 8 7 6 5 4 3 2 1

For my sons,
Andrew and Evan,
and for your generation—
may you find cherished spaces
for listening to all our stories

When you find the truth, what are you going to do with it?

—Chris Leith, Hereditary Chief,
Prairie Island Dakota Indian Community
(1935–2011)

Contents

Stranded

EVERY GOOD ROAD TRIP HAS A FEW UNEXPECTED mishaps and wrong turns. Not always a bad thing; getting lost can introduce us to new places and perspectives we might not have seen had we stuck to the original plans. That's what happened to me when I began working at the Minneapolis American Indian Center in 1995. So far, this journey has no final destination.

New lessons and perspectives continue to emerge, like the time a few years ago my engine cut out one hundred miles north of the Twin Cities while heading back to St. Paul after a weekend visit with friends on the White Earth Reservation. My father's hand-me-down old Chevy sputtered and then went silent, giving me just enough time to steer onto the shoulder of the freeway and come to a stop. Cars, trucks, and SUVs whizzed past, shaking my rickety legacy. I stared out the window and pondered the next move. Flip open my cell phone and call AAA? Wait for a highway patrol to find me? I couldn't decide. I'd fallen into a momentary deep freeze, that numb place where animals take shelter when on high alert.

Staring out the front dash, I noticed tall trees lining both sides of I-94. I had broken down in the middle of a forest. Not a pine tree forest like the ones in a Grimms' fairy tale. It was March and the branches on these trees were bare. Sweeping the late-winter sky like upside-down brooms, these trees looked familiar.

Maples.

I recognized them because I had just spent the past two days helping my friends during their annual maple sugaring. Weeks earlier they had made an offering to their mother maple tree and then hammered metal spigots into the trunks of a neighbor's sixty-foot-high maple trees. Next they hung large white plastic buckets off the spigots. As the sunlight returned, the sugar water warmed up, ran down the trunks, out the spigot, and into the buckets. When I arrived it was time to empty them. We had hopped into my friend's car and driven to the neighbor's maple grove. Walking through a layer of mushy snow into the woods, we unhooked the full buckets and carefully set them in the car.

Driving slower this time, we crossed back over the road and poured the precious contents into a large cauldron nestled over a fire in their backyard. The sweet water began its alchemical transformation. First it boiled outside until half the liquid was gone. The remainder boiled a second time on the stovetop inside their cozy house. Before leaving, my friends had gifted me with a Mason jar filled with this refined topaz nectar.

The maples outside my stranded car seemed taller than the ones up at White Earth. Surely, sugary water dripped along the highways inside their long trunks. Had anyone befriended them this year?

Then it hit me.

I hadn't broken down in the middle of nowhere. I had broken down somewhere very specific.

The numbness lifted. I dug through my wallet, located the roadside emergency number, and dialed AAA from my cell phone. Then I settled in awaiting rescue.

This forest of maples was my father's family, the Murphys' origin point in Minnesota. Our American genesis.

My hand-me-down Chevy had died less than ten miles from the homestead my great-great-grandparents had claimed 150 years earlier.

For most of my life I knew next to nothing about this place or about these distant relatives. I didn't even know their names. I knew only the same shadow story most Americans with European ancestry like me know about our past. One, two, three, four, or more generations ago family members had pulled themselves up by the bootstraps and passed their profits on to the next in line. My great-grandparents had left these woods and headed to the cities in search of work. First to nearby St. Cloud and then to St. Paul. I grew up with evidence of their pathways to success. I saw my father's father and his father's imprint in the domes of the Cathedral and the Capitol. I knew the streetcar line my great-aunt took to work in an office downtown and the name of the high school where my grandmother taught English on the East Side. I knew the parish churches where these relatives had married, prayed, or been buried from.

Their backstory? Nothing.

It had been wiped clean away, felled from my family like so many others in this nation.

I only knew that my nameless immigrant ancestors were from Ireland and they had left after the Potato Famine. I didn't know where they were from on their native island, and I certainly didn't know if they longed for home once they got here. It was as if they'd been airlifted to America in Glenda the Good Witch's bubble, spreading amnesia like fairy dust into the woods.

Where had my ancestors left our story? I can only imagine. One fragment may rest in the harbor at Cobh as they boarded a Famine ship. Another may be tucked into the cloak of a body thrown overboard. Perhaps another bit of their story sits underneath a cobblestone lining the hills of East Boston. Or held within an alcove on the steamships they traveled up the Mississippi River to St. Paul. If their muted terror, handcuffed with grief and shame, ever made it to these woods in Minnesota, I never heard it.

I knew only that my family was not unique. We had been taught not to look back. We had been trained to disconnect from family and our homelands. We had swapped our stories for a dream.

Not so in other times, in other places, in other communities. The Irish even have a story about the importance of storytelling. There once was a fellow, this story goes, who was stranded outside on a blustery night. When he tried seeking shelter at a nearby cottage, the traveler was turned away. His crime? He didn't have a story to share. Only later when he returned with an account of what he had discovered in the raw night did the traveler gain entry to the cottage.

Within this Irish worldview, living without a story means you risk exile, fated to live beyond the boundaries of belonging and survival.

As I sat waiting for the tow truck to arrive, vehicles whipped past me going sixty, seventy, eighty miles an hour. There was nothing abstract about the story. I wasn't just stranded by the roadside; my family had been exiled from Ireland.

Long before this weekend of collecting sap, I had begun looking for my family's origins. The search had turned up a second story that had broken down over the past 150 years.

When my family erased our exodus story, we also erased the story of the people whose lands we claimed in these maple woods.

My family, and this nation, had replaced it with a pernicious fantasy that neglects the true story of our Native American hosts and their land. We still neglect this missing story.

The result?

Ignorance.

I knew that the maple woods outside this stranded car once belonged to my ancestors, but I didn't know that they had also been home to at least three American Indian tribes long before immigrants began arriving on this continent.

The result?

Separation.

Even today, our communities live in exile—exiled from the land, from home, and from one another.

This breakdown, in knowledge and in connection, requires so much more than calling AAA. To survive we need to find, and then share, our interlinking stories.

So I began digging, digging below the shrouds of silence on both sides of the ocean. It has taken decades. I am grateful for the many books and libraries where filaments of the truth were stored. Yet the greatest resource has been the many good-hearted people who shared their stories and wisdom with me. I spoke to family members, historians, and elders. I listened to activists, elected officials, and grandmothers. I visited with Native people, Irish people, and those of immigrant stock like me. I am indebted to them all.

Each time I listened, new facets of understanding surfaced. Truths and untruths shone in the embrace of the powerful act of storytelling. Sometimes what I heard was so painful I wanted to turn away and give up. Sometimes it was so confusing that I wanted an authority to tell me some singular ultimate truth so I could be done with this quest. But it didn't work that way.

The pathway to story, and to belonging, had to unfurl inside me. No one could unbraid for me the dream story I'd inherited. No one could rebraid the new truths I was beginning to hear from the other side of silence. Every American can take this journey, learn from mishaps that arise along the way, and discover their own way home. For me, it took walking back to the homestead ten miles from this very breaking point to gently tap the trees so the stories they held could finally flow free.

OLD STORIES

The Cedars

SOME DANCERS WAIT IN FULL REGALIA. MANY STAND in street clothes. Others carry beaded gear over their arms. There are grandmas, little children, and every age in between. Grand Entry starts shortly. Everyone wants to get to the floor. But first the dancers must register. Patty Sam mans the registration table here at the Minneapolis Thanksgiving Celebration Pow-Wow. One by one, the dancers sign her log according to their age and dance category. Then Patty hands each dancer a numbered wristband. At the end of this spectacular event, they will return to the table for a small stipend.

I'm Patty's sidekick. As the line and impatience grow, I want to jump in and do something. Tell the girls in the middle of the line that they don't need to register—they're under age seven and automatically qualify for the $5 tiny tot stipend. Hand a pen to the quiet gentleman who has let a boisterous group of teens get ahead of him. I try to keep quiet, but if it's urgent I say something. I also let the dancers know they can double-check my answer with Patty when she's free.

In the months leading up to the event, I have written letters, reports, and grants on behalf of the volunteer powwow committee. But while this three-day powwow is under way, my job as a non-Native is simple.

I sit and listen.

It's taken me years to learn how. To learn not to dominate. To learn not to jump in and "fix" things. In fact, this class isn't over. There's no diploma or final exam. I'm still unlearning the American conqueror's code that erases Native people out of their homelands.

My education started right here where the powwow takes place today, the Minneapolis American Indian Center—the unofficial hub of the Twin Cities Native community. In fact, the Twin Cities has long played an important role in indigenous issues around the country and even the world.

The Thanksgiving dance registration table sits at the far end of the gymnasium, just to the left of the head table where Patty's husband, Herb Sam, and the head emcee, Dave Larsen, preside. From this vantage I have a wide-angle lens on the music, color, and motion ricocheting across the crowded gym. I understand that this celebration does not belong to me; still, I can love it with all my heart.

I do.

The spacious gym has transformed into a festive commemoration filled with a thousand mostly Native people dancing, drumming, snacking, chatting, singing, admiring, and catching up in the wooden bleachers that line two walls. Ten drum groups composed of men of all ages—from toddlers to elders—are seated around huge wooden drums that line the base of the bleachers. A cheerful dancing turkey mascot hangs on the northern wall, above the head table where Herb and Dave officiate. In the seating area for elders, volunteers serve swamp tea and doughnuts and shoo away younger kids trying to sneak underneath the temporary cordon. One of those elders is Valerie Larsen. Valerie is in charge of the Royalty Competition—annual tryouts for three youth dance titles.

The main attraction, however, is the gigantic orange floor where this year's arena director, Shawnee Hunt, monitors the action, enforcing protocol. Stamped into the middle of the floor is the circular logo of the Indian Center. For three days dancers step, fly, and move together around this circle.

From my seat at the dance registration table I shiver as a drum group's song leaps in time to the heartbeat. I smile watching the family helping a toddler into her dance dress. The little one is already tapping her feet even though her dress is only halfway on. An older fellow with a neatly shaven face and cowboy hat decorated with a bandanna and dangling feather at the head table registers his drum group. A middle-age woman fiddles with the turquoise belt on her buckskin dress, while moving in time with the spiral of dancers circling around the dance floor. Like the settlers at the first Thanksgiving on American soil, I am here as a guest of the powwow chairs, Herb and Patty Sam. We met through a mutual friend. Though Patty and Herb hail from two Ojibwe reservations—one in central Minnesota and one next door in Wisconsin—for decades they lived in Minneapolis.

Herb's kindness is apparent from the first moment you lay eyes on him. He's a tall man with a huge smile and mischievous eyes. Seeing his lively steps and his quick wit, no one would know that Herb is already an elder himself. Perhaps it's his vocation—a traditional healer—that keeps him so robust and good-hearted. From his perch at the podium overseeing every detail of the powwow, he radiates a sense of safety and well-being across the dance floor.

Patty is tiny—tiny frame, tiny voice, tiny hands and feet—but there's nothing small about her. Without a speck of gray hair, she looks younger than I am, but she's at least a decade older. Age has not diminished her energy one bit. One year she single-handedly cut up a deer donated by a community member for the pow-wow feast. And if you're going through a hard time, she's the first one who'll tell you that the Creator never gives us anything we can't endure and so you can and will too.

The Minneapolis American Indian Center rests in a low-income residential neighborhood just south of downtown Minneapolis and a mile west of the Mississippi River. This gathering place was built in 1974 when I was in seventh grade. Stitched together from multistory panes of concrete, wood, and window, the building's sharp surprising angles and geometric shapes express joy and delight. Facing Franklin Avenue, the front of the center features a gigantic wooden mosaic created by the famous abstract artist George Morrison. Morrison was a member of the Grand Portage Ojibwe Tribe even farther north than Herb or Patty's tribal communities.

The wood Morrison chose for this prominent community sculpture is cedar, a tree sacred to many Native tribes in North America. Cedars are also the oldest trees in Minnesota. A grove of cedar more than ten thousand years old lives in the northeast corner of the state.

Just as the cedars carry on an ancient legacy, so too do the drummers, singers, and dancers here at the pow-wow. As Lisa Bellanger, daughter of an American Indian Movement (AIM) founder, told me, "It really takes a lot of study to learn the diversity of our singing traditions. But we don't have a choice. It is said that when the drum is sounded, it's like a breath of life. The drumbeat gives life to the people. It calls the people and the spirit together to be one heart and one spirit. It also carries messages into the future. So it's our responsibility to help children learn the songs to sing into the future."

The younger generation doesn't take this responsibility lightly. The traditions they are learning are never just about themselves, but about taking care of the community and carrying forward its legacy.

"I listen to the drum and follow the drumbeat when I dance. I feel really good then. I dance for my people. I dance for my brother who died. I dance for my family, and for healing when we have problems," a ninth grader told me after he was crowned Brave Minneapolis, one of three Royalty titles that Twin Cities' Native youth compete for each year at the Minneapolis Thanksgiving Celebration Pow-Wow. The new Miss Minneapolis said, "I am really proud to keep the traditions of our ancestors alive so that Native culture won't die out."

The Thanksgiving Pow-Wow is not my first foray into the Minneapolis American Indian Center. In the mid-1990s, I worked here for a youth program called Ginew/Golden Eagles. I've been working in the Native community ever since, writing grant proposals for funding, preparing reports to program partners, and sometimes helping write curriculum.

I'll never forget the first morning I arrived at the Indian Center.

I turned off Franklin Avenue into the side parking

lot, switched off the car, and stared hard at the two-story wall of windows that wrapped around the building. I wondered if I *should* go in. Sure, I'd been hired, but did they really want me, a White woman, in there?

I feared that if I stepped through the tall wall of windows, I would get thrown out.

As I sat in my parked car, I noticed a stand of bent conifers with a reddish hue to their skinny trunks that lined the parking lot. No one I've asked is certain what they are, but my best guess is cedar, the same wood of the George Morrison sculpture around the front of the building. These cedars looked like they belonged up in the northern woods, not on Franklin Avenue in the middle of the city.

How could I—great-great-granddaughter of pioneer immigrants—dare walk into the Indian Center? The cedars intimidated me as if suggesting, "Go home. Go back where you belong."

Where *did* I belong?

I had grown up less than two miles from the Indian Center. Just follow Franklin Avenue, across the river, and up the hill to the oak-studded neighborhood. There, middle-class residents like my family live in Victorian-era wooden houses decorated with bay windows, wraparound porches, and leaded-glass doors. The streets wind around the hill like peelings from an apple. On the summit of our hill, an old water tower reigns over the neighborhood, keeping watch like a crenellated castle keep.

The view from the top of Tower Hill offers a panorama of our urban river valley—of both downtown Minneapolis and downtown St. Paul. It gives a glimpse of the confluence of the Mississippi and the Minnesota rivers. The panorama stretches farther still, out beyond the horizon where our land knits together the western prairies, the central hardwoods, and the northern forests where the ten-thousand-year-old cedar trees still live.

As a child, I had been taught that all this land belonged to me.

To the east stood the buildings of downtown St. Paul, known by the red "1" on top of the First National Bank building. To the west stood the buildings of Minneapolis, made recognizable back then by the Weather Ball, an ever-changing colored globe atop the North-western Bank that forecast the coming weather. To the north, in the direction of my maternal grandparents' prairie farm, lay land, land, and more land.

Our land, my land.

Closer at hand were the landmarks that made up the boundaries in my triangular neighborhood. On one side the railroad yards and flour mills belched and burped day and night, turning the grains from the prairies into flour. On the second side a new interstate freeway called I-94 connected Minneapolis and St. Paul to points farther north and south. At the base of our triangular neighborhood ran the Mississippi River. We could see but not hear trucks rushing on the freeway and barges humming on the river taking our flour and iron ore to points east and west and south all the way to the Gulf of Mexico. From this urban river valley, we sent these crops out across the seven seas. The flashing bank signs in both downtowns signaled that their vaults were flush from the deal.

Here on this hill in a midwestern city, I belonged to this river and the land, to the commerce and the sounds that connected us to the farm and to the rest of the world.

But throughout my childhood, I had never once gone down the hill, over the river, and into the Indian Center. No one in my family or school or neighborhood had a relationship with the Native community. Instead, we lived by a code of segregation, straddling two sides of the river, of this land.

We didn't even see the first people of this land from the top of Tower Hill.

Was this blindness a choice? Or were we truly unaware of our Native neighbors?

Sitting in the parking lot outside the Indian Center that first day, the feeling of dominion on the hill vanished.

Was it my land, after all?

Showing up for work at the Indian Center required me to reconsider my domain. It asked me to rest a while in an awkward discomfort, that raw wedge of space in the gut that often Americans prefer to ignore. Hidden there was the embarrassing but fuzzy recognition that non-Natives have some unpaid debt to Native Americans. That morning, I couldn't ignore it any longer.

I didn't drive away. Instead, I walked into the Indian Center and slowly began to uncover a different way of understanding what it means to be an American in this land. A way not of dominion or banking the resources of the land. Not one of separation and segregation.

Rather, I was invited to join a circle.

A circle that unites all people with the land, just as the drum unites the dancers, the singers, and all generations with the beat of the heart.

In those first few years of working in the Native

American community, I slowly began to glimpse this circle through the diverse ways my colleagues connected to one another, to their lineage, and to the land. My colleagues beaded cradleboards to carry their infants as generations of mothers had done before them. They sewed regalia and danced at powwows. They introduced themselves not by their cities or their states but by their tribe. They told stories of their ancestors who had defended their lands or lost their lands. Often, humor was the antidote to loss. The more I listened, the more I learned.

Sometimes the lessons cost me my pride.

Early on at a meeting on the youth curriculum at Ginew/Golden Eagles a colleague said, *Oh, so you're the expert who's going to tell us what to do.*

I remember fidgeting with my glasses and squirming with discomfort inside. I waited for someone else to talk. In that painful silence my heart broke open.

For the first time in my life, I was being called out for my assumption of dominion here at home. I was being asked to stop, slow down, and investigate the view from Tower Hill.

I began asking tough questions. I knew that my great-great-grandparents were Irish and that they had farmed in Minnesota, but that was about it. I didn't have names for them. I didn't know where they had homesteaded land.

Working at the Indian Center moved me to ask who they were and how their lives connected to my own.

Next I began to wonder whose land *had* my great-great-grandparents homesteaded when they arrived in Minnesota? Had they taken land that my colleagues' ancestors had defended? That of my Ojibwe friends on

the Thanksgiving Celebration Pow-Wow committee—
Herb, Patty, and Valerie? Land that belonged to the arena
director's Ho-Chunk ancestors? Maybe my ancestors'
homestead belonged to the Dakota, the tribe of the emcee Dave Larsen and the oldest tribe in the state.

Unlike my colleagues in the Indian community, I
also didn't know where my ancestors had come from
in Ireland. I didn't know their beliefs or customs. Their
foods or their dress. Or how they carried their infant
children. I didn't know whether the Irish language
sounded like the rolling hills and hawthorn hedges of
home.

As a child I had once asked my paternal grandfather
where our family came from in Ireland. I'll never forget
his response. A judge on the Minnesota Supreme Court,
my dad's father was comfortable making declarations.
Sitting in a covered armchair by the fireplace, he dis-
missed me sternly. "We're just Potato Famine Irish."

Without a clear story or lineage, I have often felt
suspended midway between Ireland and America with
no place to land. An African American friend of mine
could hardly believe me when I tried to explain this
rootlessness soon after I started working at the Indian
Center. "But you *are* the culture," she insisted when I
told her of my quest to search for my ancestors' land
back in Ireland and right here in Minnesota.

She was right—the dominant culture was mine for
the taking. With my college degree and family connections, I could have picked nearly any combination of
education, career, or lifestyle I wanted. A corporate career and a lake home, or nonprofit work and a used car?
I had picked the latter, working for twenty-five years as
a writer for community-based nonprofit organizations

like the Minneapolis American Indian Center. Still, my children and I have shelter, a home in the capital city of St. Paul. We have basic needs and add-on luxuries available to us. But what lineage would my sons carry on?

Where are our ancient cedars?

For the past twenty years, I've explored these questions of lineage and land. Of belonging and home. The answer for me—descendant of faceless Irish Potato Famine immigrants—is more a practice than a final solution: listen. Listen to the land, listen to one another. Slow down and reach into the uncomfortable spaces ignored for centuries. Touch the wounds in our hearts and the earth. Show up with courage. Set down dominion. Step with kindness.

It's not complicated, really. Just watch the dancers. Follow the circle.

The Crab Apple

THE QUEST TO DISCOVER MY FAMILY'S LINEAGE HAS not been easy. It's taken me almost two decades to find names and places for ancestors in Ireland. To uncover whose Native lands my Irish Potato Famine folk had taken. None of these stories was simple to reconstruct, none without pain. Yet the facts were relatively easy to find. Learning to let go of the American story line that lodges people and the earth in harmful hierarchies was harder, much harder than fact-finding.

This challenge is not over. I'm still learning.

Each new piece of evidence unearthed in this journey forces me to rethink how I view the world. It challenges me to let go of the stance of dominion I learned as a child growing up on Tower Hill.

One fact emerged quickly in the research into my family's story. My great-great-grandparents on my father's side had homesteaded 160 acres in the central hardwoods of Minnesota, about a hundred miles northwest of the Twin Cities. In 1858, the same year Minnesota became a state, they traveled with a company of fellow Irish immigrants who named their new home after the virgin maple grove they claimed and cut down. The Maples, ten miles from the spot where I broke down in my father's old Chevy.

Perhaps this is why trees have accompanied every step of the way in this journey back in time, starting with the cedars at the Minneapolis American Indian Center and landing right back at my home just across the river in St. Paul at the crab apple tree in my front yard. My connection to this tree is not so much a historical fact needed in this quest. Rather, it holds clues to the worldview of dominion I inherited. A worldview and legacy I will pass along to my children unless I choose to shake it off.

When I bought my house in the capital city of St. Paul, this narrow urban rectangle was a miniature Garden of Eden. In the front, a garden of native shade plants and a thick hedge of perennial iris and peonies made a pretty entrance. At the back of the house edibles lined the alley—a tiny vegetable plot, fat rhubarb leaves, and a pyramid of strawberries. Raspberries and blueberries bounded the property to the north. To the south stood a wooden gated trellis that led to the side yard where a chokecherry stood, guarding a galaxy of tulips and daffodils that blossomed every spring.

The crab apple tree in the front yard was the jewel in the crown. When we first moved here in 2002, this tree was a perfectly balanced Y. Its center trunk grew five feet before splitting into two main branches that rose another twenty feet in the air.

A "woman" tree, my friend Becca had said before she moved up to White Earth. Each leg of the Y flowed into supple fingers stretching skyward in prayer. In May, this balanced web danced in a crown of pink blossoms.

By midsummer, the blossoms had transformed into tiny garnets—rosy-red crab apples. In the fall, orange-hued leaves hugged the branches tightly and then let go, modeling gracious surrender. No matter the season, even in the thick of winter when only the skeleton of bare brown branches remained, the crab apple pressed a perfect half-circle halo into our urban sky.

Not anymore.

Thunderstorms, squirrels, and gaggles of boys raised on this block for multiple generations have taken their toll. Half of her is nearly gone. One sultry summer, my oldest son was hanging out in the tree with friends. He was playing in a rope ladder tied around one of the two main branches. All of a sudden he fell. Though he only dropped a few feet, the impact was huge. Almost half the tree collapsed. The next year, lightning slashed more of the main leader.

Today the crab apple leans to the left like a one-legged elderly woman. It takes effort to really look at her. The tree's broken half sprouts a few limp suckers. But no amount of foliage will cover her stunted form, just as makeup never really disguises an older woman's wrinkles. The human eye often turns away from the jagged, the torn, the loose ends, away from death. We revere youth. We prefer a beautiful tree, like a tree on the shoreline reflected on a river at dusk. When these two trees, one in the sky, one in the water, sew themselves together into a perfect circle in our hearts, we breathe easily.

My crab apple offers no such ease. Her vulnerable skeleton reminds us that death is just outside the door.

Now in my fifties, life's twists and turns have left me vulnerable, too. At the half-century mark, death and decay are no longer just imagined. I can see them clearly in the mirror. I haven't lost half of my body like the crab apple tree, but gravity is taking its toll. The skin on my arms is starting to droop. The lines around my eyes look a little like an old-fashioned pioneer doll whose face is carved from dried apples. Still, as far as I know, no one is contemplating terminating me.

Not so with the crab. I could hire someone with a chain saw to remove the crab apple. Once removed, I wouldn't have to look at her listing forlornly. I wouldn't have to be reminded of death with each step out the front door.

What will be my apple's fate?

Apple trees appear in stories all around the world—China, India, Mexico, Greece, Arabia, and Ireland. From Eve's apple in the Garden of Eden to the 1904 American adage "An apple a day keeps the doctor away," these stories relate the transformative power of the apple. Many Americans are familiar with the story of Johnny Appleseed, but a lesser-known apple story comes from Henry David Thoreau. Thoreau delighted in the domesticated apples of New England, apples descended from fruit trees brought by British colonists to America. Yet he wasn't satisfied. He craved sighting a wild apple tree. The native crab apple. He writes:

> Our wild apple [in New England] is wild only like myself,
> perchance, who belong[s] not to the aboriginal race here,
> but [has] strayed into the woods from the cultivated stock.
> Wilder still, as I have said, there grows elsewhere in this
> country a native and aboriginal Crab Apple, "whose nature
> has not yet been modified by cultivation." It is found from
> Western New York to Minnesota. . . . They are remarkable

for their delicious odor. The fruit is about an inch and a
half in diameter, and is intensely acid. Yet they make fine
sweet-meats, and also cider of them. . . . "If only cultivat-
ed, it does not yield new and palatable varieties, it will at
least be celebrated for the beauty of its flowers, and for the
sweetness of its perfume."

So in 1861 this famous American writer traveled by rail and steamboat to Minnesota. Landing along the Mississippi River near Minneapolis, Thoreau immediately set out to find a local guide to help him hunt down a wild apple.

I had never thought of any tree, let alone my crab apple tree, worthy of so much effort. A cultivated cousin to the indigenous wild crab that Thoreau searched for, the crab in our front yard was just an ornament. Our jewel in the crown. I am embarrassed to admit that I have never even made use of the fruit on the crab.

Now it is too late.

When she was healthy, her rosy garnets littered the front lawn beginning in early August. The grass and front walk were covered so quickly that heading into the house became a game of chance—could you make it to the door without feeling a crab apple squish underfoot? Rather than gather the fruit and make jam or jelly, I'd rake up the apples and dump them into the garbage bin behind the garage. Why had I distanced myself from the tree and its bounty? What lens did I wear that placed this "fine sweet-meat" beneath my consideration?

The answers may lay two blocks away, inside my maternal grandmother's old kitchen. Unlike my father's relatives, who had migrated to the Cities in the early 1900s, my maternal relatives had stayed on their farms in the prairie lands of the Red River Valley until after the Great Depression. My mom's parents had raised two daughters in a little yellow bungalow just two blocks from my house and this crab apple here in St. Paul. My grandfather worked at the nearby Ford plant that hugs a bend on the Mississippi River like a fortified castle. My grandmother, who had trained as a hospital nurse, had stopped working. In the postwar era of modernization, she stayed at home. She watered thick beds of petunias, ironed the sheets, polished the silver, and cooked meals for her family on their new electric range.

Though they are no longer alive to ask, it is possible that my grandparents knew this very crab apple tree on my front lawn. Most fruit trees max out at thirty to forty years. Through careful tending small fruit trees can live more than one hundred years. I don't know how old my crab apple tree is, but when I first moved here an elderly neighbor told me that "this is the oldest tree on the block." My house was built in 1900, but surely the elderly crab isn't that old. Say it was planted in 1950. Then the tree would be a decade ahead of me, just over sixty years old and definitely alive when my grandparents still lived two blocks away. If my mother's mother had known this crab apple tree, had marveled at its pink fragrant blossoms each May, it wouldn't have been her first.

My grandmother's childhood on the prairie farm up north had introduced her to fruit trees long before she was a married woman in a midwestern city on the Mississippi River. She and her sisters would ride horses out into the small wild fruit stands that grew out of the rare soggy bottoms. In skirts, they'd trudge out of their buggy into the tall grasses and prickly bushes to pick stubborn plums and tart crab apples and fill their metal pails. I can imagine my grandmother and her sisters, the three Murphy girls, laughing as they gathered fruit under the hot summer sun. They'd gossip about the boys they hoped to meet at Bachelor's Grove at the dance the next weekend, or cuss under their breath when they got a gash of blood from the thorny bushes they traipsed through to get back to their horse. They'd eye one another as if to say, "It's a good thing Mother didn't hear you."

Scratched, sweaty, and sunburned, they'd ride home and carry the filled buckets into the huge kitchen of their white clapboard farmhouse. The next day, they'd wash and boil the fruit, adding precious white sugar and pectin. Under their care, the bitter fruit transformed into light pink sweet syrup that they packed in sea green jars. They put the jars on wooden shelves lined with browning newspapers that told of Temperance and flapper girls and the price of a bushel of wheat. Through the long white winters, the crab apple jelly reminded the Murphy girls of summer and sun and dreams of boys and dancing and the worlds they hoped to make manifest.

These days, farmers rarely gather the earth's bounty by hand and in company like my grandmother and her sisters. Ever since World War II, farmers have fled the farms into the cities in search of an easier life. Those who stayed on the land turned farming into big business. Instead of the 160 acres my father's family had homesteaded in The Maples, or the 360 acres my maternal relatives farmed farther north on the prairie, a farmer today needs thousands of acres to survive. The result is that very few Americans ever touch the earth any longer.

Most of us have never plucked a wild plum. Or made crab apple jelly.

My maternal grandmother's story parallels this exodus from the farm and into the cities. When she was twenty, she left her position teaching in a one-room schoolhouse on the prairie and took a bus to Brooklyn, New York, where she earned a nursing degree in the middle of the Great Depression. After she graduated, she moved to the Twin Cities and reconnected with my grandfather, an old sweetheart from the prairie. He too had left the family farm to work in the big city, packing not jellies but mechanical parts of the American Ford.

Along the way, my grandparents' generation grew disenchanted or perhaps ashamed of the simplicity of life on the farm. My grandmother didn't teach her own daughters how to make jams and jellies. By then, store-bought jams and jellies available at the grocery store had replaced old-time communal activities like making jam in the farmhouse kitchen. The daughters of the American pioneers now gave their daughters the luxury of leisure time and modern convenience. My mom didn't have to gather or boil or pack fruit. My mother didn't have to dirty her hands to dig potatoes out from the earth's brown nest or smell the sting of overripe crab apples pecked away by worms. Instead, she listened to the radio, dyed her hair blonde, and drove around the city with her friends in her convertible, a gift from her father the ex-farmer.

When they retired, my mother's parents moved back to their farm. Yet it was there, on childhood visits each summer, that I learned of my grandmother's disdain for things old and raggedy, for wild things. After the six-hour drive from Minneapolis, my siblings and I would file into our grandparents' newly built ranch house, drop our suitcases near the pull-out couch in the lower level, and snack on her home-baked cookies and Country Time lemonade in an immaculate kitchen. Then we'd run back outside to play on the tire swing my grandpa had set up in an apple tree for us, practice shooting tin cans with his hunting rifle out behind the grain bins, pull a sampling of sweet-smelling carrots from the huge garden, and hop on my grandfather's golf cart to tour the new trees he had planted around their 360 acres of prairie gold.

Sometimes we would pile into the backseat of their Lincoln Town Car to visit the relatives on nearby farms. My grandmother and mom would sit in the front. In the backseat, we kids fell under the spell of the soothing sound of gravel sputtering against the rubber tires. I'd lean into the back window and breathe in the hot dusty air and marvel at the wide wheat fields under the vast sky. I'm not sure if my grandmother appreciated the beauty of the prairie any longer. Yes, she'd returned at fifty to what she knew as home, the prairie where the patchwork of homesteaded farms were pieced together in a profitable tapestry. Yet the way she held the steering wheel with one hand and a lit cigarette in the other signaled that this drive was just an ordinary drive.

But for me, a city girl, every stitch of dancing wheat, every farmhouse, every shelterbelt—rows of columnar trees planted in straight lines by pioneers—felt precious and blessed. The infinite sky was taller than any building back in Minneapolis or St. Paul. It was longer than the Mississippi River that divided the two cities. The hot summer sun rolled east to west across the sky like a minute crystal in an immense chandelier—one tiny detail in a much grander scheme.

As we drove into this ocean of air, the farms cropped up out the rear window at regular intervals—separated by the 160 acres that the original pioneers homesteaded. Every once in a while we'd pass an abandoned farmhouse. These slanted wooden structures, more dead than alive like my crab apple, sagged into the earth. Who had these houses once sheltered? I wondered as we whizzed past, gravel whirring under the weight of the car. My grandmother was less curious. "They ought to set a match to that thing," she'd say as her cigarette ash spiraled out on the wind. Maybe she wished she was back in the yellow bungalow in the capital city where she didn't have to remember the wildness of the land. Maybe she wanted to pass on the pioneer's hard-won practice for survival: take control of the land and put it to work. Break up the prairie sod. Blacktop the dirt road. Fill in the ditches. Fence in the cows. Keep wildness at bay. She could, like millions of other Americans, go to the grocery store and buy what she needed. She didn't have to touch the earth any longer.

This is my grandmother's legacy. Separation from the earth was her gift. This is the worldview I could pass on to my sons.

We, the sons and daughters of the European immigrant pioneers, are no longer connected to the land. We don't step kindly on the earth. We practice dominion. We believe we can do anything we want with the land and keep both life and death at a distance. We won't let the prairie return to the wild, for if we did, we would have to admit frailty, death, and defeat. We would return without form, back into the earth and wind and sky and waters from which we all came. We would all be wild.

This inheritance keeps me at an eerie distance from the crab apple on my own front lawn. It is partly why I could so easily sweep up the tart rosy orbs and dump them into the garbage rather than collecting them into a big black pot on the stove to boil and bubble into a sweet sticky syrup for jam.

Yet it is only now that the tree is dying that I perceive this distance between me and the crab apple in this Walden Pond—my front lawn. Thoreau writes of the wild apple tree he sought in Minnesota: "These are the ones whose story we have to tell."

This crab apple tree asks me to reconsider my worldview. Rather than distance myself from her or gloat like a queen atop Tower Hill, my crab apple tree begs me to come back down to ground level, to stand beside her and acknowledge death. Yes, I need the facts of this land and of my Irish heritage, but until I stand still and listen, I will never relearn how to touch the earth. I will never reconnect with its beauty and with its sorrows. To begin the descent down Tower Hill, I revisit two powerful stories known both to me and my grandmother.

The Pines

MY GRANDPARENTS DIDN'T ACT ALONE; THEY had been taught since childhood. Take the stories of Paul Bunyan and Laura Ingalls Wilder. These two storytellers have educated generations of Americans into the world of dominion and separation. For those of us in the Midwest, both stories are close to home. Laura's stories tell of her pioneer childhood in Wisconsin, Minnesota, and the Dakotas. Paul is the iconic American woodsman whose strength, endurance, and size we admire. Many states, including Minnesota, claim Paul as their own good guy.

My first memory of Paul Bunyan takes me back to my grandparents' farm on the prairie. On long summer days when we weren't driving to check out sunflower and soybean fields, visiting the cows on our cousins' farm, or eating ice cream cones at the general store in town, we'd stay inside to get out of the sun. My grandmother was a big reader, so I'd browse her bookshelves, landing often on the books my mother and aunt had read as children, like *Little Women*. Another book that caught my eye was *The Wonderful Adventures of Paul Bunyan*, the 1945 version of the iconic American lumberjack retold by Louis Untermeyer. Every summer, the beautiful etched drawing on the cover jumped out at me from my grandmother's antique-stained bookshelf. Today, I know this evocative artist to be Texan native Everett Gee Jackson, who copied the style of Mexican muralist Diego Rivera. Jackson's wide but gentle swathes of geometric shapes gave Paul an ironic softness. On the cover, Paul Bunyan is etched in a rainbow of forest greens and pictured as a gigantic baby dressed only in diapers. He is lifting a huge wooden cradle overhead, stomping through a village and across a lake that are both smaller than his feet. This giant baby fascinated me as a girl—how did he ever fit anywhere? I wondered.

Inside the 1940s book about our American lumberjack, each chapter begins with a brown pen-and-ink drawing showing Paul at different stages of his life—from the time he burst out of his cradle to the time he and his ox Babe plowed right through a lake. In one illustration, he is dressed in boots, pants, a checked flannel shirt, and an old-fashioned brimmed wool cap. Paul holds an ax that is so big that he needs both hands to grasp it. Beside him are four columns—gigantic tree trunks that are taller than he is. A few men, dressed in similar gear, work nearby but they are only as tall as Paul's boots. Chips of wood fly out into the woods from Paul's ax. Down go the woods.

Every summer I also revisited a postcard tucked inside this book. Written in sky-blue ink, the postcard is addressed to my mother and her sister at their yellow bungalow two blocks from my dying crab apple tree. The writer was my great-aunt Helen who had inherited the prairie farm where my grandmother grew up making jams and jellies. The very same farm where my grandmother learned to cut and trim and mold the prairie.

On the front of Helen's postcard is a photograph of a huge sculpture of Paul Bunyan and Babe the Blue Ox that still stands in the northern Minnesota town of Bemidji. The postcard is dated 1946, the year after the Untermeyer book was published and the year my mother turned eight. Helen writes to her nieces just after the girls' annual visit to the prairie farm: "Dear Girls: Here is the card that I think maybe you would like to put in your scrapbook or keep it for you to show your friends. Hope you got home without any trouble. Write to us soon."

I loved reading and rereading this note, not so much for the content, but for the chance to imagine my mother as a child. At that time, I still imagined my parents as giants with mythic powers. I couldn't believe they had ever been young and vulnerable. What I didn't realize was that every summer I pulled *Paul Bunyan* off the shelf, I was also absorbing the assumption that the woods and the land were ours for the taking.

Though the town of Bemidji, Minnesota, claims Paul as their own, no one knows for certain where this American hero was born. In his retelling of the legend, Untermeyer writes, "Some of the old people say he was born in Maine. Some say in Minnesota. Or in Michigan. There are even some who claim he came out of the pine woods of Canada. But they all agree that his name was Paul Bunyan, that he was the hero of the Northwest, and that he grew up to be the biggest thing in the whole country."

His description of the wooded northland reveals

just how vast the virgin forests of North America once were:

> *He was building himself a house in Minnesota, a house that was so high that the last five stories had to be put on hinges to let the moon go by. This was the country for Paul. Trees and trees and trees. Pines and maples and oaks for thousands of miles, from the Great Lakes clear through the Northwest right out to the Pacific Ocean. Here were trees so wide you'd get tired walking around their trunks, trees so high it took an ordinary man a whole week to see to the top of them.*
>
> *"Here is where I make my home," said Paul. "This is a country to grow up in. But what am I going to do for a living?"*

He wandered under the trees looking for an answer. He found it in the woods. Paul did not much like the pine trees in the forests of North America. Or perhaps they didn't like him. Untermeyer writes:

> *But the trees whispered among themselves, mocking the young giant. The heavy branches seemed to gossip spitefully when he went by; there was always laughter in the leaves, and it seemed to Paul that they were laughing at him.*

Laughing at him? Yes, for Paul these American trees had "spiteful" energy. He didn't like being laughed at. No one does. In Paul's case, the trees made him feel vulnerable. Certainly a conqueror doesn't want to admit feeling the tremor of fear. Neither does a bully. They often respond by acting out in anger and rage. In Untermeyer's retelling, Paul destroys the trees:

> *So Paul left the woods and went up to the Mesabi iron range and dug up some metal. Then he heated and hammered it*

into two bars. Then he welded the bars together and sharp-
ened them into an axe. Then he walked back into the forest
and picked out the tallest tree.

"Now let's see what this axe can do"—and it seemed
to Paul that all the trees stopped talking and only the little
leaves kept up a sort of frightened whispering.

Paul forges a battle-ax and starts chopping until he's ex-
erted his dominion over all the pines in the Minnesota
woods in a war he's only imagined. He stops when the
trees are nearly silent. Like an abuser, he doesn't stop
until his rage transmutes their voice to a "frightened
whispering."

The scarier truth is that Paul didn't act alone. His
story and imagined war helped fuel and justify the mass
execution of this nation's northern woods.

❦❦❦

Minnesota is home to fifty-two kinds of native trees.
Our top ten trees, in reverse order, are sugar maples,
balsam fir, red maples, cedar, tamarack, black ash, paper
birch, balsam fire, black spruce, and in the number-one
position, quaking aspen—thin white-columned trees
with spade-shaped leaves that whistle in the wind.

Trees account for 16.3 million acres of our entire
land base, making up one-third of the state. Who stewards this bounty of trees? Industry accounts for just
7 percent of our trees and private landowners own
about a third of our trees. The remaining 60 percent,
nearly two-thirds of Minnesota's trees, is held in trust
by local, state, and federal government. Nearly all of
these trees are second growth. That means they've been

replanted—largely by logging companies that contract with the state to manage our publicly owned forests. Like my farming relatives on the prairie who clearcut crops of soybeans and sunflowers at the end of the summer, the loggers cut down the trees as if they were planted in huge fields. After they finish, they replant. The only difference between the loggers and the farmers is that it takes more than one year before their next crop will be ready for harvest.

One of the people who has been chronicling the changes in our midwestern woods is David Mladenoff, a professor at University of Wisconsin–Madison. Mladenoff traces his interest in our woods to his experience growing up in a former mining town in Michigan. During his childhood, the town's economy died because the riches in the earth had been tapped out. The Paul Bunyans of the mining industry had extracted all the iron for their battle-axes until nothing was left to take.

As a teacher, Mladenoff has inspired graduate students who are also studying the impact of the loss of our woods in the Upper Midwest. They write that "the mixed conifer-broadleaf deciduous forests of this region experienced logging that at the time was globally unprecedented in its speed and intensity, with over 20 million hectares deforested in 60 years." Despite ongoing reforestation efforts, the great woods of Minnesota, Wisconsin, and Michigan experienced an overall 27 percent decline in conifers between 1850 and 1990. In fact, only two trees have experienced an upsurge since the logging era—maples and quaking aspen.

White pine was the most popular tree in the Paul Bunyan logging era, accounting for almost 75 percent of the trees felled during the logging heyday. Mladenoff's students write:

> Lumbermen preferred white pine for two reasons. First,
> white pine floats. When rivers functioned as highways,
> pine's buoyancy enabled timber men to move logs cheaply
> from the forest to the mill and then to markets. Second,
> white pine was an excellent building material, because it
> grows into tall boles of clear wood that are easily worked,
> flexible, light, yet strong and durable.

Mladenoff's students estimate that 315 billion board feet of white pine was harvested from Michigan, Wisconsin, and Minnesota between the mid-1800s and 1930s.

Where did all this pine go once it was cut and trimmed and sent downriver to the lumber mills of Minneapolis and Milwaukee? Scholar William Cronon reveals where in his book *Nature's Metropolis: Chicago and the Great West*. He argues that the white pine cut from the Lake Michigan drainage basin built Chicago and the cities and towns that stretched out across the Great American plains. In Minnesota, the lumber of our north woods built our cities and towns, too. I am not exempt from this war against the woods. That Victorian dollhouse in Minneapolis where I grew up, built from the 1902 Sears kit? The 1900 home where my boys and I now live in St. Paul with a dying crab out front? Both homes were built with the boughs of slaughtered north woods trees.

American environmentalist pioneer Aldo Leopold warned that the loss of the forests meant much more than just the loss of trees. It meant the loss of all the beings that live in the woods. Like Thoreau a century before him, Leopold shared his growing understanding of nature in a personal memoir about a piece of land he cared for—an old farm in northern Wisconsin. Leopold published *Sand County Almanac* in 1949. Though it's taken decades for the American public to catch up to his wisdom, Leopold understood the interrelatedness of bioregions. He wrote that with the loss of trees came the potential loss of "350 birds, 90 mammals, 150 fishes, 70 reptiles, 1000s of insects and plants." Leopold also understood that to restore this diversity and richness of the forest, one needs to do more than just protect a single species. In *Sand County Almanac*, he critiques preservation efforts that focus on only protecting a single species: "We console ourselves with the comfortable fallacy that a single museum piece will do, ignoring the clear dictum of history that a species must be saved in many places if it is to be saved at all."

Minnesota has a few such natural display pieces. The most famous of these is a virgin red pine in Itasca State Park—not far from the statues of Paul and Babe the Blue Ox that appeared on the old postcard written to my mother and her sister. There are a hundred lakes within Itasca State Park. The headwaters of the Mississippi trickle out of one of them. Islands of forest surround this watery land, including the virgin red pine. Separated by a wooden guardrail, our statuesque pine stands on display like a mannequin or an act in a freak show at the state fair. It is about three hundred years old and stands 126 feet high.

Alone and guarded, this pine is not healthy. Nor are humans, if we separate ourselves like a museum piece from the rest of creation.

❦❦❦

If Paul's story taught generations of Americans—including my grandparents, my parents, and me—that the woods were ours to be killed, Laura Ingalls Wilder taught American schoolchildren that the woods we destroyed were empty. I was first introduced to Laura and her family's log cabin during the late 1960s. The Vietnam War was in full swing and our fourth-grade teacher had been called away from the classroom on special assignment in the National Guard. While he was gone, the substitute teacher read aloud to us during a cold spell in Minneapolis that kept us inside during recess. Under the fluorescent lights that hung in parallel rows above our Formica desks, I listened—we all listened—to Mrs. Bachmann read *The Little House in the Big Woods*.

Blizzard winds blew outside our tall classroom windows. I could feel the snow melting on Pa's beard as he hugged Laura after a trip to town. I could taste the sweetness of the hard maple sugar packets he brought home. I could hear the wind coming into the chinks between the wooden logs, when Laura lay tucked under the quilt at night.

I longed for more of Laura's world that winter. I went to the traveling bookmobile every Thursday to borrow and read all nine books in the series. By Easter vacation I had convinced my mother to take me and a friend to a fabric store and buy several yards of dark green plaid cotton, black thread, and a simple dress pattern. Several days later, we had sewn our own pioneer dresses. We wore them around the neighborhood with dedication. As the spring days warmed into summer, the long sleeves and long skirts grew hotter and itchier, but I refused to give up my make-believe pioneer world. Instead, I elaborated. I found an old sheet in the attic that I turned into a sunbonnet and apron. I found an old pair of skates in the basement and unscrewed the blades and wore them as lace-up boots. I hand-stitched a quilt for a newborn cousin.

When I lifted the scratchy green plaid dress up over my arms and stepped into my make-believe past, I thought everyone wanted to be a pioneer like my hero Laura. It is only now many decades later as a homeowner who trims my front lawn as neatly as Paul trimmed the entire north woods that I am beginning to see that not everyone would want to play Laura. Certainly not my colleagues in the Native community. Laura and Paul displaced the ancestors of my friends and colleagues at the Minneapolis Thanksgiving Celebration Pow-Wow, who belong to the state's three major tribes—the Dakota, the Ojibwe, and the Ho-Chunk.

Herb and Patty Sam are Ojibwe, a tribe that followed a spiritual prophecy to the northern lakes and woods of Minnesota more than five hundred years ago. Today the Ojibwe are the most populous tribe in the state. They have seven reservation communities in the northern half of the state, but many Ojibwe live in the Twin Cities. That's because in the 1950s and 1960s, U.S. federal relocation policies coerced Native families to leave their home reservations and move into urban centers like Minneapolis.

Shawnee, one of the powwow arena directors, is Ho-Chunk, a tribe whose ancient homeland is in the deep cliffs and caves of neighboring Wisconsin. So too was my colleague at the Indian Center who called me out for being "an expert." To clear land for families like Laura's in the Big Woods of Wisconsin, the U.S. government removed the Ho-Chunk from their homeland in Wisconsin to Minnesota. Then in 1862, the Ho-Chunk were forcibly packed off to Nebraska.

Powwow emcee Dave is Dakota, and the Dakota are Minnesota's oldest community, our first people. Minnesota, or Mni Sota, is a Dakota word meaning land of cloudy water or land where the water reflects the sky. Mni Sota Makoce is the Dakota ancient homeland. Their sacred birthplace is at the confluence of the Mississippi and Minnesota Rivers, not far from my crab apple tree in St. Paul. This whole urban river valley is the Jerusalem, the Holy Land, of the Dakota. More than twelve thousand burial sites—graves and mounds—are thickly spread across the state, like millions of stars in the sky on a dark clear winter night. While gliding up the Mississippi River in 1846, the English painter Henry Lewis commented, "The countless mounds, enthroned on the hilltops like monuments of a long-gone race, form an immeasurable cordon along the blue horizon."

Minnesota's remains are not only numerous, they are extremely old. In an interview with Hamline University anthropologist and former state archaeologist Barbara O'Connell, I learned that there are only a dozen human remains that are at least ten thousand years old in the United States. Two of these ancient people, almost one-fifth of America's oldest-known humans, were found in Minnesota.

Nevertheless, it's almost impossible to find stories that feature contemporary Dakota, Ojibwe, and Ho-Chunk, or their ancestors, who lived in the woods long before Laura or Paul arrived. Here in the Twin Cities—home to the sacred birthplace of the Dakota—there's just one historical marker. It appears overlooking the Mississippi and Fort Snelling, accessible to the hardy few who bike the river cliff path. This lack of information is partly due to missing facts. It is also the result of how we are trained to see the world. Through story.

It's not too late to reexamine the assumptions within the stories we pass along generation after generation in America. It's not too late to shrug off the blinders of dominion and omission rooted inside Paul and Laura's stories.

When my oldest son turned four, he received a boxed set of the Little House in the Big Woods series. I remember opening the inky-smelling paperback to the first page, excited to read to him at bedtime that summer. We started at the beginning—the opening passage in *The Little House in the Big Woods*:

> Once upon a time, sixty years ago, a little girl lived in the Big Woods of Wisconsin, in a little gray house made of logs. The great, dark trees of the Big Woods stood all around the house, and beyond them were other trees and beyond them were more trees. As far as a man could go to the north in a day, or a week, or a whole month, there was nothing but woods. There were no houses. There were no roads. There were no people. There were only trees and the wild animals who had their homes among them.

Then I stopped. Were Laura's woods empty of people? Were Thoreau's at Walden Pond? Leopold's in Sand County?

Not at all.

These famous storytellers had forgotten the people in the woods. The Dakota, the Ojibwe, the Ho-Chunk, and five hundred other tribes that make up this land we call America. I took a chance and paused at the end of that first chapter and told my four-year-old son about our land's first people. But that was just the beginning.

In this quest to find my family's origin story, a quest that began with the cedars at the Indian Center, the tale of omission, the story line of dominion resurfaces everywhere. It takes constant attention to not stumble on these old roots. It requires not just finding facts but also seeing in a different way. It requires us to rethink our old stories, even stories we cherish.

In this different worldview, humans are not "museum pieces" separate from other people and the land, like the virgin pine tree on display in the state park up north. White people like me are not kings and queens reigning over the land, as I learned to do on Tower Hill. We too are a part of the web of earth and sky and water and air. As I adjust my lenses to this new way of looking at the world, I wonder what I might find and feel if I dare revisit another revered American story. The story of our first Thanksgiving.

American Chestnut

LAURA'S BIG WOODS, PAUL'S PINES, AND MY GRAND-parents' legacy that taught me to distance myself from the land and the people are sequels to a much older story. A story that began in the 1400s with the kings and queens and popes of Europe. In America, we repeat a version of this story every November with the retelling of our nation's Thanksgiving myth. Native and non-Native had agreed to be friends, right?

Unlike Laura and Paul, the Pilgrims and Squanto hadn't lived in our big woods. Their story took place half a continent away on the eastern seaboard. In high school, I had learned that Massachusetts was the epi-center of American history. After all, Boston is where the American Revolution started, where Paul Revere took his midnight ride, and where the first Tea Party took place. It's where the *Mayflower* landed. It was on the books. History with a capital H.

After college, I had moved to Boston to live with friends and get closer to what I believed to be real History, away from the provincial stuff of potatoes and pi-oneers. I ended up staying and marrying a man who grew up a few blocks from the Lexington Green and could trace his ancestry back to the *Mayflower*. Though we are no longer married, our sons' lineage now includes this chapter in American history.

When I had a chance to go to England in 2009, I decided to take my oldest son. Together we would revisit the story of the Pilgrims—a European American story and his story, too. We visited Plymouth, the seaside harbor in southern England from which the Pilgrims had set sail in 1620. Like reading about Laura Ingalls Wilder's empty woods when my son was much younger, the trip forced us to rethink how we tell our American story. It turns out that not everything that happened with the Pilgrims made it into our history books.

At the Plymouth train station, we two—mother and son—hoisted backpacks and strolled toward the seaside hostel where I'd booked a room. We traveled a path that led under a highway, along Plymouth's main street lined with little shops, past a multistoried department store and a cinema complex hidden behind ornate white stone. Eventually, the brick path stopped at an elegant seaside park with a promenade overlooking the sea. This park featured huge sculptures, including one named after Britannia, Britain's first lady—who some say is modeled after Boudica, an indigenous woman warrior who led her early British tribe in a defeat of Roman conquerors. Another sculpture profiled Sir Francis Drake, the intrepid sea captain who from this same harbor led the British in their own quest to conquer the world. Sir Drake is credited with helping England overtake Spain as the world's leading naval power and for bringing the British into the international slave trade. These two achievements, some claim, formed the foundation for British colonialism beginning first with their neighbors to the west in Ireland.

After snapping photos of the larger-than-life sculptures of Drake and Boudica, Andrew and I turned around and faced the sea. What I saw amazed me.

The Plymouth harbor is a gentle bay, protected by the rough cliffs of Cornwall to the west. By the time these wilder cliffs bend around to Plymouth, they soften and roll sweetly toward the tame coastal hills of Dorset. Everything about the supple sea, the wide-open sky here, said, "You are welcome."

Andrew and I turned left, continuing along the promenade in the company of seagulls hawking their syncopated song overhead. We passed old bathhouses with empty swimming pools and memorials to war veterans and headed to a sheltered quay filled with tourist sites. I kept wondering why people would ever want to leave this protective, gentle harbor and conquer the rest of the world. The tourist museum on the quay at the end of the promenade answered this question in a single word.

Profit. Even the Pilgrims wanted money.

As American children we are taught to believe that everyone aboard the *Mayflower* was a Pilgrim and that they left England to pursue religious freedom. In fact, the iconic *Mayflower* ship did not even belong to the Pilgrims. It belonged to the Plymouth Company that bought and sold goods between England and America. They happened to have room available on their trading ship that year. The Pilgrims were stranded in Plymouth because the first two ships they'd tried to set sail on had leaked, so they had had to turn around. Though there was room on this third ship, the *Mayflower*, the remaining 102 Pilgrims didn't have any money to pay for their steerage. What they could do was broker a deal by selling their future labor and crops. So before the Pilgrims boarded the *Mayflower*, they made a deal to work for the Plymouth Company in America.

This third time was a charm: the *Mayflower* did make it across the Atlantic and the Pilgrims made it ashore. They planted themselves in a recently abandoned farming village named Pawtuxet. Pawtuxet faces the Atlantic Ocean near the tip of Cape Cod, about a hundred miles south of Lexington and the Battle Green.

The abundant chestnut tree greeted the Pilgrims when they arrived on American soil. Native to Europe, Asia, and the Americas, the American chestnut was once so plentiful along the Eastern seaboard that they numbered in the billions and accounted for a quarter of all the coastal trees. It bore nuts that once fed many creatures, including deer, turkey, bears, and passenger pigeons. Later these nuts became famous in the opening lines of the yuletide classic "The Christmas Song": "Chestnuts roasting on an open fire."

The chestnut woods and abandoned village that the Pilgrims claimed was home to the Pawtuxet, an indigenous band belonging to the Wampanoag tribe. Squanto, the famed friend of the Pilgrims, was the last remaining Pawtuxet. Up until a few years before the Pilgrims arrived, the Pawtuxet and other Wampanoag bands had lived throughout the cape. However, a horrific plague, probably smallpox carried to their village by earlier European visitors, had wiped them out. When the Pilgrims arrived, they found untended cornfields, caches of corn seed, tools, and houses.

Edward Winslow, one of the Pilgrims, describes the homes in Pawtuxet: "The houses were made of yo[u]ng Sapling trees, bended and both ends stuck into the ground; they were made round, like unto an Arbour, and covered downe to the ground with thicke and well wrought matts, and the doore was not over a yard high, made of a matt to open; the chimney was a wide open hole in the top, for which they had a matt to cover it close when they pleased; one might stand and goe upright in them." The eastern trees literally welcomed the Pilgrims home to Pawtuxet: the outer mats and doors were made from the ubiquitous American chestnut.

Today the American chestnut is almost extinct.

The Pilgrims appropriated everything they found in the abandoned village, including the homes gracefully woven together with the central hardwood trees. Then the Pilgrims prayed for thanks at their luck. They would need more than luck to survive, however. By the spring of 1621, with fifteen lost on the voyage over and forty-five dead by the end of winter, only forty-two Pilgrims remained.

Ric Burns's series on American Indians and the American West taught me what really happened over the next decade. The neighboring Wampanoag tribe, led by a highly esteemed chief named Massasoit, had kept a watchful eye over the Pilgrims ever since their arrival. The Pilgrims weren't the first Europeans they had encountered; both the French and the English had arrived to trade goods and disease—probably including the smallpox that had wiped out the Pawtuxet. None of the previous European visitors had ever stayed on like the Pilgrims. That first winter, Massasoit noted their sickness and hunger, and so in the spring he and Squanto paid them a visit. Then they decided to help the Pilgrims. In exchange for corn seed, land, and furs, the Wampanoag would get European trade goods: knives, kettles, and drills to more easily make wampum, their valuable currency made from seashells.

At first this reciprocal relationship benefited both the Pilgrims and the Wampanoag. To acknowledge these benefits, a small party of Wampanoag did come to the Pilgrim camp that second November and offered their visitors five deer. It is this gift and the meal that they shared that day—not turkeys—that is the basis of our first American Thanksgiving. It took place in Pawtuxet, not Plymouth. The exchange was spontaneous, not planned, as we tell ourselves. It was an offering, a gesture made by the Wampanoag. The indebted Pilgrims did not invite the Wampanoag to their table.

Two years later the Pilgrims decided to go to war.

In 1623, Myles Standish, a Pilgrim and the Plymouth Colony's military commander and treasurer led an attack on a Wampanoag village. The village attacked was home to a neighboring tribe, the Massachusetts. When the warring Pilgrims returned to Pawtuxet, they carried the head of one of their Massachusetts victims, a war strategy the English had practiced a few decades earlier in Ireland. Word of the Pilgrims' barbarism reached the Wampanoag leader Massasoit. Massasoit's generosity shifted to a new strategy—not alliance but defense.

Meanwhile, the Pilgrims and fellow colonists arriving from England continued to expand their territory and their wealth. By the 1630s, the Pilgrims had finally earned back enough to repay their debt to the Plymouth Company—and then some. They had enough cash to purchase the company that once held them ransom and established the Massachusetts Bay Colony. Thousands of English came and settled in the area, forming modern-day Boston.

This is not the history that we revisit every year in our American Thanksgiving myth. It's not quite what makes it into our history books. It is only now, many decades after leaving school, that I learned about what happened next, thanks again to Ric Burns's amazing documentary that brought this untold story forward in film. The Wampanoag and the other northeastern tribes suffered gravely from the Pilgrims' actions. Worse than war were continued outbreaks of smallpox. Worse than smallpox was the land grabbing that decimated the tribes' capacity for self-sufficiency. If they did not have land, the eastern tribes could not hunt or farm.

By the 1650s, the tribes faced another threat: missionaries who exchanged food for prayers. Inside the walls of so-called praying towns the Wampanoag were forced to testify in front of a panel of ministers that the Christian God was angry with them and then forced to shed "tears of repentance." Even Massasoit, who fought back as long as he could, was eventually forced to sell his tribe's lands and pay tribute to the God of Genesis and to the Pilgrims, the community he had kept alive back in November 1621.

Massasoit's son Philip was not willing to give up. He took over his father's leadership role within the Wampanoag and led a coalition of tribes into a war. By then nearly half of the indigenous peoples had been removed to praying towns. Rather than be forced to read the Bible in exchange for food, Massasoit's son demanded land and the right to practice their own spirituality. For more than a decade, Philip led his coalition in attacks against the growing English colony—from modern-day Massachusetts to Connecticut, New York, and Rhode Island, where English settlements and colonies had sprung up. Though Philip's army did have some successes, it was overpowered by the weaponry of the English. Those captured were sold into slavery in the West Indies to work the sugar plantations. By 1676, Philip retreated and, like his father, no longer freely led his people in their own land.

This is not the happy Thanksgiving myth we renew each year at Thanksgiving. War, starvation, disease, cruelty, disrespect, tyranny. And yet what happened next is even more outrageous. Philip was murdered, dismembered, and decapitated. His head was displayed in an annual celebration in Pawtuxet for two decades. His son, Massasoit's grandson, was sold into slavery and exiled to the West Indies at nine years of age—younger than either of my sons.

This gruesome story is one that we do not tell our children. We teach just the opposite, a giddy morality story of equal exchange between the Pilgrims and the Wampanoag. We did when I was a child, and we continue to do so today in our history books and through every grade-school Thanksgiving feast reenactment—something that my youngest son was forced to do only a few years ago here in St. Paul.

In the place where this continent met the eastern sea, the Pilgrim's desire for profit had overturned the natural human bonds of compassion. Then why do we promote a lie about the Pilgrims and the Pawtuxet and Wampanoag? Was profit the only motive driving the Pilgrims and the English colonists to commit such horrid acts of terror upon their hosts in Massachusetts?

Who said genocide was okay?

ᴠᴀᴠᴀᴠ

I wasn't finding the answers in American History with a capital H. To keep unraveling the roots in our American story, I had to look elsewhere. I decided to call the Mille Lacs Band of Ojibwe tribal offices and ask to speak to the tribal historian. Out of the eleven reservation communities in the state, I had picked Mille Lacs because it is closest to the Twin Cities, but it is also the tribe to which powwow chair Herb Sam belongs. Their historian answered right away and agreed to meet a few weeks out.

On the appointed day, I headed north out of the Cities and made my way to the tribal office building at Mille Lacs. The Mille Lacs reservation is named after a lake by the same name. Mille Lacs is so wide and deep that you can't see across it or down to the bottom. It is rich with walleye and wild rice. Though the Ojibwe live here now, the Dakota made their home here for thousands of years earlier, evidenced by ancient village sites around the lake. The Dakota name for the lake was Spirit Lake, or Bdewakanton or Mdewakanton. It's clear that the Mille Lacs Ojibwe Band have continued to be good stewards. Not only have they protected gravesites of the Dakota; they have also used a new resource to care for the community. Casinos.

Ever since gambling was made legal on Native reservations, a new myth has sprung up declaring that American Indians are now rich. Not so. There *are* a handful of very wealthy gaming tribes in the United States, but they are also known to be very generous. The Shakopee Mdewakanton Dakota Tribe in Minnesota is one of these, and they donate $27 million annually. The majority of tribes don't earn enough from casino profits to address systemic poverty on the reservations.

Most tribes funnel what they do earn right back into the community. At Mille Lacs, for instance, the tribe uses gaming revenue to build and maintain Ojibwe language schools for the young and nursing homes for the elders.

The tribal office shows this same kind of care. It's a one-story octagonal building. Inside colorful floral borders reminiscent of Ojibwe beadwork wrap around the ceilings and are stamped into the floor. At a round welcome desk, a woman greets me. I ask for Don Wedll, the tribal historian. Within no time, a tall man appears and takes me into his office down the hall. After I briefly explain the purpose of my visit, to understand the true story of the land, Don jumps in with an American history lesson I'd never heard before.

"It all begins with the Doctrine of Discovery," he says.

"What's that?" I ask the tribal historian while sipping the coffee he's offered me.

The English, he explains, were not the first colonial power that had reached the American continent. Other seabound nations, including Portugal and Spain, had preceded them in a quest for gold here in the Americas. These European nations found justification for invading, killing, and raping the people and lands through the words of their spiritual ally—the Catholic Church.

The Pope, the chief Catholic storyteller, we could say, put forth the first of several stories, or papal bulls, proclaiming European rights to land outside their continent. In 1455, Pope Nicholas declared that Portugal could claim lands in West Africa. Then in 1493, Pope Alexander VI declared that Isabella, the queen of Castille, Aragon, Sicily, and Granada, had the right to ownership of all the islands and lands her explorers discovered. "That's the Doctrine of Discovery," Don explains. Once "discovered" and named, the land was declared as property of the Catholic kings and queens of Europe.

The territory the Pope gave the European monarchs was vast. The 1493 document declares:

> We give, grant, and assign to you and your heirs and successors, forever, together with all their dominions, cities, camps, places, and villages, and all rights, jurisdictions, and appurtenances, all islands and mainlands, found and to be found, discovered and to be discovered towards the west and south, by drawing and establishing a line from the Artic pole, namely the north, to the Antarctic pole, namely the south, no matter whether the said mainlands and islands are found and to be found in the direction of India, or towards any other quarter.

"The English weren't going to be outdone by the Catholics on the Continent," continues Don.

No, I think to myself, especially not after Sir Francis Drake defeated the Spaniards from a ship launched from the serene harbor in Plymouth. So the British followed suit with their own declaration of dominion. The English part of the story begins when King Henry VII hired John Cabot (formerly known as Zuan Chabatto) to sail to North America more than one hundred years before the Pilgrims and the Plymouth Company landed in Pawtuxet.

According to an 1884 history of American public lands, "The English, by reason of the voyage of the Cabots along our eastern coast in 1498, acquired the title of first discoverers to the country extending from the thirty-eighth to the sixty-seventh degree of north latitude. They were instructed to discover countries unknown to Christian people and to take possession of the same in the name of the King of England." Not only did they claim the land; they made sure that whoever was there first no longer had a hold on it. The Doctrine of Discovery "gave an exclusive right to extinguish the Indian title of occupancy, either by purchase or by conquest."

As I listen to Don continue to explain the backstory to American history within the walls of this circular building on tribal lands that have been cared for by Minnesota's indigenous peoples for thousands of years, I try to process what he's telling me.

With a myth like the Doctrine of Discovery in place, the English kings and explorers, the Pilgrims, and the Massachusetts Bay Colony believed they had the right to take the Wampanoag land. They also believed they had earned the right to convert them to Christianity in the praying towns they built around Boston. And how did they earn it? Because their Christian God said so. The pope and the king granted them dominion, and they took it.

"You know, the Doctrine of Discovery isn't just a dusty law sitting on some ancient library shelf," Don warns. "It's still on the books. And in this country we've added to it. Just given it a different name. Names, really. The Marshall Decision and the Ninth Article of the U.S. Constitution." He fills me in. In 1823, U.S. Supreme Court Justice John Marshall declared that Natives had lost "their rights to complete sovereignty, as independent nations." Instead, they had only the right of "occupancy." The United States maintains this dominion in our constitution's Ninth Article, which states, "The

United States in Congress assembled have the sole and exclusive right and power of regulating the trade and managing all affairs with the Indians not members of any of the States."

This is conquered land.

When our conversation ends, I thank Don Wedll for this history lesson here on the shores of Mille Lacs, of Spirit Lake. He has been so generous with his time and knowledge. I want to do something in return, but I can't think what. As he nods good-bye, I wonder if a part of him suspects I will turn out to be just another Pilgrim—grabbing what I want and causing harm to the people and the land.

Driving back to the Cities, I reflect on the hidden layers of American history. From the myth of Thanksgiving to the Doctrine of Discovery, our centuries-old stories ensure that we never really see the conqueror's sleight of hand. Like the American chestnut that once housed the Wampanoag and greeted the Pilgrims who sailed from the serene Plymouth Bay, most of this story has disappeared from view. Yet when you keep unwinding the baton of time, unravel the sturdy roots in the story of dominion, the truth becomes clear. We never had an agreement to be friends in Pawtuxet.

But if this land is conquered, even my tiny plot in the capital city of St. Paul, who is the conqueror? Not distant Europeans like Pope Nicholas or John Cabot. Not officials like Myles Standish or John Marshall. My hunger to know my lineage, my family's story, forces me to keep looking. Who were the conquerors closer to home? Here in Minnesota where I live with my two sons and a dying crab apple tree?

The Elm

TURNS OUT THAT THE CRAB APPLE ISN'T THE ONLY dying tree in my city lot. An elm that stands on the boulevard—that rectangular strip of public land between the street and the sidewalk—isn't well.

"It's got the blight," said a young fellow in a white hard hat on the morning the city tree workers arrived to take it down.

"The blight?" I asked. Like the blight that destroyed the American chestnut, or the potato blight that sent my Irish ancestors packing from Ireland to North America 150 years ago?

"Dutch elm disease," he answered, backing away from the mechanical lift that was rising up into the air toward the crown of the elm.

I thought Dutch elm disease had come and gone in the 1970s, but it continues to plague trees in regions east of the Mississippi. A European beetle carries a fungus that spreads along elm roots. The fungus clogs the vessels that carry water to the trees. Elms literally die of thirst.

Sometimes I feel parched, too. My thirst isn't for water like the elm trees. I long for connection. Ever since I started working in the Native community and learned about my colleagues' ancient ties to the land, language, and traditions, I've felt cut off at the roots. From Ireland—my family's ancestral land.

Perhaps this thirst for a lineage is the conqueror's curse. Once Europeans arrived in America, they gave up their ancient homelands. Not just *they* as in John Cabot or Myles Standish. *We*. My family.

Me.

Growing up I never had considered myself a conqueror. Conquerors and colonizers were kings and queens, the Pope and the English. My first inkling that this title also belonged to me came a decade before I started working at the Indian Center. I was halfway across the world teaching English in Indonesia.

After marrying the man with Pilgrim roots in the mid-1980s, we headed to Jakarta to teach English for a year at a private language school. Just forty years after independence from centuries of Dutch colonization, this capital city was not only crowded; it was also extremely polluted and poor. By American standards, our teaching salaries were modest. But by Indonesian standards, we were rich.

One day I was walking through the market near our house toward the local taxi stand. All of a sudden something hit the back of my calf. I turned and saw a banana peel at my feet. A group of men started laughing and someone shouted a word I didn't understand, "*Belanda! Belanda!*" I turned around and stared back. The men, the women, the vendors, the barber all looked back at me. For one strange moment the market was completely silent. No one said a word. I didn't either. I crossed to the other side of the square and hopped into a taxi as quickly as I could.

When I got to my destination—Hotel Indonesia—I found my fellow English teachers, ordered up a gin and tonic, and relaxed by the pool for the rest of the afternoon. It was there that I learned what the word *Belanda* meant: Dutch person, or colonizer. Though I didn't want to admit it right away, my accusers had been right. I had all the privileges the Dutch once had, siphoning off the resources in Indonesia for my own benefit. I was a twentieth-century colonizer.

In America, it is harder to acknowledge the same truth.

If it had taken me a decade to realize that other people—the Dakota, the Ojibwe, the Ho-Chunk—had lived in the central hardwoods of Minnesota before my Potato Famine Irish ancestors arrived, it took me yet another decade to realize that my family and I were conquerors, too. Are conquerors.

My ancestors didn't settle along the eastern seaboard where Massasoit and his nation still haunt the Boston Harbor. My ancestors didn't head across the plains and western mountains to settle in the high wet homelands of the Pacific Northwest tribes. Nor did they settle in the South, taking the fertile swamps of the Cherokee and the Choctaw, or the desert rainbows of the Hopi and the Apache. No, my ancestors journeyed thousands of miles across the Atlantic Ocean and claimed 160 acres of maple trees in the American Midwest. To the home of three American Indian nations—the Dakota, the Ojibwe, and the Ho-Chunk—the tribes to which my fellow volunteers at the Thanksgiving Celebration Pow-Wow belong.

I didn't know my Irish ancestors who left Ireland to escape another blight and make a new home in the American woods. We had no names, no faces. As my paternal grandfather, Judge Murphy, explained, we were just invisible Potato Famine Irish.

If I were to finish unraveling the maze of dominion in America, I would need to cast a line back across the Atlantic Ocean to Ireland.

꧁꧂

I'll never forget the Saturday morning when my youngest son and I were sitting on the kitchen floor playing with measuring cups, graters, and Christmas cookie cutters spread across the white linoleum. The phone rang. I picked it up and heard a deep voice on the other end of the line. My father.

"Let's meet down at the river for a walk. In about a half an hour?"

"Great," I answered. "At Randolph?"

"Sure. Don't forget to bring that short guy with you. And remind me. I've got something for you."

At the river, our trio headed down the black tar path lined with yellowed oaks and rusty maples enjoying the beauty of the autumn day. Before the walk ended, my father handed me a large white envelope.

"It's a family history. Maybe it will help you on your search," he said, explaining that it came to him by way of his brother, their cousin in St. Cloud, and a more distant cousin in Michigan—a relay team skipping like stones along the Midwest and its rivers.

Later that night after both boys fell asleep, I opened my father's gift. Flipping through the document, I searched first for my father's father, my grandfather Murphy who had told me that we were only Potato Famine Irish. His name appeared where I expected—

54

seventh child of my great-grandmother and my great-grandfather, a stone cutter who had helped build the cathedral of St. Paul.

Now where? I turned the page, walking deeper into the past. A great-great-grandmother's name froze, then glimmered on the white page. "Katie Hughes must have come from Ireland about 1845. She married John Meagher in Boston. John and Kate came to Minnesota and settled at The Maples in Stearns County."

Katie Hughes Meagher, mother to my great-grandmother, grandmother to my grandfather Murphy. My great-great-grandmother?

I whispered her name over and over again. Katie Hughes Meagher. Katie Hughes Meagher. As I spoke, my heart sprouted a raw tendril, growing like a greening spring day and reaching back in time. It was so soft and so vulnerable that it almost hurt the way that looking at a newborn infant can make one want to weep.

Inside the tender sprout I recognized my desire to connect, to belong.

The conqueror's thirst.

Then I returned to the first line of the document—a line I had skipped.

"Michael Hughes—Mary Ryan—Knockahopple, County Tipperary. Married sometime in the 1820s." I pieced together the outline of our story. In the early 1830s, my great-great-grandmother, Katie Hughes Meagher, was born to a Michael Hughes and a Mary Ryan in Knockahopple, County Tipperary.

We have a place, too? I *can* claim a native land?

I stared at the old family history and tried pronouncing the name of our village. Knockahopple.

For the next month I searched for the birthplace

of my great-great-grandmother, on maps and online, but to no avail. When I found a link to an e-group for local Tipperary history, I sent off a query. Six months later, I received several responses. One said there was no Knockahopple. A middle-aged woman who ran a lovely bed and breakfast near Knockahopple urged me to come visit. Another wrote me in confidence, pleading that I not divulge his name, confirming that there is a Hughes family still living out at the old homestead in Knockahopple. He confided, "Knockahopple means 'horse hill,' but it's a lonely place."

Finally, almost a year after my first query, I received an e-mail confirming that a Michael Hughes was indeed related to my great-great-grandmother, Katie Hughes. This writer included Michael Hughes's postal address in Knockahopple. More parched than ever, I sent a letter back across the salty Atlantic Ocean:

> Dear Mr. Hughes,
>
> I recently received a letter via electronic mail from a Mr. Pakie Ryan suggesting that our families may be related. I am writing to find out!

After describing what I knew about our family history, I continued:

> If fate should have it that we are in fact related, my father and my whole family would love to hear from you. Please write as soon as you can! Thanks so much for your time.
>
> Most sincerely,
> Nora Murphy

Two years later a postcard arrived. From Ireland. A St. Patrick's Day card featuring a stone monk's cell and decorated with neon green shamrock stickers. The author was Anna Hughes, the wife of the mysterious Michael Hughes. She had received my Christmas cards for the past two years and apologized for not replying sooner.

"Yes, we are related," she wrote. Her husband, Michael Hughes, and my father are distant cousins, both nephews four generations removed from Katie Hughes Meagher.

The shamrock shore was truly a part of my past.

After two visits to Knockahopple since receiving that first note from Anna and Michael, many severed roots have been reconnected. Now when I introduce myself, I can say where my family comes from. I can claim an ancestral land.

But did my great-great-grandmother know she was taking someone else's lands when she sailed from the shamrock shore?

I've never seen a photograph of Katie Hughes Meagher, yet I can picture her. I imagine her between the lines. To me, she doesn't look like an invader or a conqueror. She's not a Dutch colonial soldier sweating under the weight of his metal hat in the equatorial sun of Java. She is not a slave trader, walking below deck with a whip in her hand. Nor a Pilgrim with a tall black cap and metal buckle at her waist. She has soft white skin, tinted red in the cheeks and her forearms. Her eyes are like my mother's—a light blue-gray that catches the morning sun and sends a ray back to you in the form of a wish for the day.

Her hair is pulled back in a tight bun, but at night when she lets it down, its brown lengths curl slightly inward at the end, like a flower petal that tilts toward its stem after a few days in a vase. Her bones are wide—hips, shoulders, no waist, just like me. She's neither tall nor short, neither fat nor thin. But she walks with the slightest limp, with her right leg being just a centimeter longer than the left one. As she ages and gives birth to nine children, this limp grows more pronounced. Her wide bones disappear under the weight of more flesh, and her soft white skin becomes wrinkled, her brown hair gray. Only her eyes remain constant over time. I imagine that when she held my grandfather as a baby, just a few years before she passed, she gave him that same ray of light—a wish for his day, for his future in this new land for which she had given up everything she ever knew.

In Irish, Katie's last name Hughes is actually Aodh. *Aodh* means fire. What kind of fire, I wonder? Fiery energy of the conquerors? Or keepers of hearth and home, like the patron saint of Ireland, St. Brigid, who used her fiery powers to transform and heal from her monastery in the oaks of Kildare. Perhaps the light that my great-great-grandmother held in her eyes was a remnant of this elemental duty to the clan and the universe, for without fire we would forever remain cold.

I imagine Katie's home fire back on the lonely Horse Hill. Born in the early 1800s, my great-great-grandmother didn't join an army, or parade a severed head on the streets of Pawtuxet. Nor did she even wear the costume of the soldier. Instead of metal hats or whips or guns, she wore an apron.

If this apron had pockets, they were probably filled

with useful things like a handkerchief, a thimble, and a flint to light the fire when the embers in the hearth puttered in the damp rains. She probably wore a long cotton skirt or dress most of her life, topped with a blouse, and perhaps some kind of cotton shift underneath. When she was lucky, she got to wear a woolen cloak in the wet and cold seasons. I know she wasn't always that lucky. For many years after she arrived in Minnesota, she didn't have a warm cloak; she shared one with her daughters. Imagine the long winters in Minnesota, the below-freezing weather, the winds coming through the cabin logs without a woolen cloak?

Did she shiver back home in Knockahopple? Maybe. Maybe not. What I do know is that Katie didn't thirst for her story as a child. She didn't feel parched for connection. My great-great-grandmother's story was woven into the very Irish landscape that reared her. She didn't have to go out searching for a lineage.

All she had to do was walk out the cottage door.

I picture Katie out walking on days when she wasn't needed to wash clothes, tend the fire, or keep an eye on the cow. There were three main destinations she and the Hughes family had around the mountain—a school, a cemetery, and a sacred well. They traveled on footpaths, which cut across fields, past old homes and stone markers, alongside swamp grasses and peat bogs. Each step brought a new gift—a hawk's distant song, diamond raindrops shining in the yellow gorse bushes, the possibility of hearing the call of a little person and luring her into the circle of hawthorns that none of the Horse Hill farmers had ever dared cut down.

Katie's school wasn't a typical school. The English had outlawed Irish education, so her school was illegal.

It was an outdoor gathering place on a cliff cut into the mountain and marked by a few large boulders and a simple rock wall for sitting. Children gathered when they could to take learning about their heritage and their stories from the great-grandson of a learned bard whose ancestors had once tutored the sons of the Kennedy chiefs, the clan that once led this part of Tipperary. The children liked listening to their teacher tell the old Irish stories on their cliff, like the one about the Milesians who had come to Ireland thousands of years ago on boats that the Tuatha de Dannan used magic to keep from landing. Or the one about the powerful woman who lived in the water and fought with death every year when the bluebells bloomed in the pasture. Or about the people who worshipped in the woods: Finn MacCool, St. Columba, and St. Brigid.

If Katie could free herself to go to school a few times a month, she traveled the route to the sacred well and the ancient cemetery even less, only on feast days. The whole Hughes family would go together. On the first of May, they would visit the sacred well to say prayers and visit with their neighbors in honor of the Virgin Mary and St. Brigid. Because their religion had been outlawed, the priest would only join them in the gathering to say a few prayers if it was safe. Outdoors and with the sound of the rushing spring at the well, the women would bring out some of the first fresh butter of the season and soda bread for a small feast. The priest would join the men for a few shots of poteen, handmade whiskey the men reserved for special occasions.

Six months later, if the rains hadn't started up too badly, the Hughes would travel down the mountain to celebrate All Soul's Day at the ancient burial remains.

Marked with upright moss-covered boulders that looking like rickety teeth, the stones jut vertically into the gray November air. Here were buried the ancestors who had lived here long before even their clan leaders, long before Oliver Cromwell and his soldiers who took their Irish land and long before Katie herself was born. This feast day was quieter than the merry May celebration by the well. For the Irish say that at this time of year, the spirits of those who've passed over visit us. The children couldn't play games or look for gold in the stream. They had to stay close by their mothers' side and pray or whisper. Still even in this silence, Katie found gifts— like the warm feeling that spread over her as they left the tombs. It was the feeling that someone was there, still watching over her after all these thousands and thousands of years.

Did these ancestral spirits follow Katie across the ocean? Radiate their warmth to her children in this land of The Maples where the ancient burial remains of another people lay buried?

I think not.

Far away from our original fires, we declared dominion.

Declare it still.

The prosperity that came of claiming the homestead in The Maples remains with us today, passed along from one generation to the next. The conqueror's linked chain went from Katie to her children born in The Maples, including my great-grandmother Mary, who married a Murphy who chiseled granite from this land to build the St. Paul Cathedral. It continued on to their eight children, like my grandfather, who served as a judge on the Minnesota State Supreme Court underneath the dome of the Capitol. The chain forwarded its privileges to my grandfather's four children and fifteen grandchildren like me, five generations removed from the rude log cabin shorn off The Maples. Today it links the sixth generation of children born from The Maples—my two sons. We have all prospered off the bounty of the original 160 acres in The Maples.

Nor are we done cutting down the trees.

The elm tree on my boulevard is now gone. Chopped, conquered by Dutch elm disease and a bevy of city workers in hard hats.

The crab apple and I shiver in the late autumn winds whipping around the front yard. I want to go inside and take cover, but this journey forces me to continue shedding the past, to clear the lenses that obscure the truth. If I am a conqueror, I need to know whose land my great-great-grandmother, the girl from the lonely Horse Hill, had taken and how.

CONQUEST IN
THE MAPLES

The Maples

LIKE LAURA'S WOODS IN WISCONSIN, THE MAPLES IN central Minnesota were not empty when Katie Hughes and John Meagher claimed 160 acres in a virgin maple grove in 1858. The Ojibwe still returned to The Maples, for hunting and sugaring, yet they were no longer welcome in their woods. There was "liable to be serious trouble before the sugar making season is over," the Princeton Union reported in March 1892. "The settlers are expecting trouble with the Indians as they still persist in spite of all the warnings. They are erecting their teepees wherever they have a mind to."

The paper also reported on conflicts that resulted in legal action. As I learned from historian Bruce White, one such conflict occurred between settler Harvey M. Bennett and the wife of John Skinaway, who "came on his land and commenced to build a wigwam .... he notified her to leave and she refused to go and said she was going to make maple sugar there on his land." Shortly after that, John Skinaway was arrested and sentenced to thirty days in "the village lock-up." These clashes took place in and around the Mille Lacs Reservation, the Ojibwe band to which powwow chair Herb Sam belongs and the closest reservation to The Maples.

In those days, sugaring wasn't just a hobby like my weekend visit to friends at White Earth. The Dakota, the Ho-Chunk, and the Ojibwe had long relied on the annual maple sugar to survive. Every year as the light returned to the land, sugaring supplemented the dwindling winter food supplies for the indigenous tribes of Minnesota.

Like my grandmother and her sisters picking wild fruit for jam, sugaring was a communal activity. In 1850, Seth Eastman, a gentleman soldier from the East Coast, painted a rich portrait of a Dakota sugar bush. No part of his canvas is empty: women gather wood, pour sap into large birch barrels, tend fires where the sap is being clarified. At a birch lodge, another woman keeps watch. This synchronicity of action takes place under the graceful, bare arms of tall, curved maple trees that nearly block the sky.

When Eastman painted this Eden within the maples, he was not a complete outsider. He had married a fifteen-year-old Dakota girl named Wakaninajinwin, the daughter of Cloud Man, a Dakota chief. Seth later abandoned his Dakota wife for a New England bride, but his grandson became a famous Dakota leader and medical doctor named Charles Eastman. In his later years, this Eastman published books about Dakota life. In one of his books, he describes maple sugaring as a child before his family had to flee Minnesota for safety:

> *The hearts of the boys beat high with pleasant anticipation when they heard the welcome hissing sound of the boiling sap! Each boy claimed one kettle for his especial charge. It was his duty to see that the fire was kept up under it, to watch lest it boil over, and finally, when the sap became*

sirup, to test it upon the snow, dipping it out with a wood-
en paddle. So frequent were these tests for that first day or
two we consumed nearly all that could be made; and it was
not until the sweetness began to pall that my grandmother
set herself in earnest to store up sugar for future use.

Ojibwe journalist Wub-e-ke-niew (Francis Blake Jr.)
described how his nation revered the same sugar maple
woods:

In my great-great-grandfather's time, old-growth forests
covered more than half of this Continent. . . . The trees rose
to meet the skies, and the sentience of these ancient living
beings was a part of our Anishinaabe Ojibway community,
part of the seamless continuity of time. They were more
magnificent than the finest of the Europeans' cathedrals, but
they were not oppressively cold, psychologically manipu-
lative man-made canyons of stone; nor flying-buttressed
edifices like hordes of giant locusts couched in waiting
to devour the land and suck the life out of Grandmother
Earth. . . . The forests were home, serene and secure, gentle
and wise. Theirs was a concert of voices: the sharp snapping
of trees in the cold winter nights, the wind in the pines,
the low calls of mother foxes to their young . . . and the
crackling of the fires in the sugar bush.

If the maples were so essential to the Dakota and the
Ojibwe, how did the pioneers like my family or the
settlers reported in the Princeton Union come to believe
the woods and the maple sap were theirs?

Pamphlets and letters reached hungry corners all
over Europe urging them to immigrate to America. For
instance, in 1855, three years before the Meaghers arrived in Minnesota, a European missionary living and

working among the Ojibwe northwest of The Maples named Father Pierz wrote: "Hurry now, my dear Germans, you who are always planning to change your location and to settle in Minnesota, do not put off embarking upon your immigration, for the sooner you come, the better settlement sites you will be able to choose."

So hurry we did. But the Meaghers and the tens of thousands of other Europeans who rushed to Minnesota for land didn't act alone. In a deceitful sleight of hand, the U.S. government continued to use multiple strategies and policies to take Native lands. Then they turned them over to European families like the Irish enclave in The Maples. These strategies included:

- Peaceful negotiations (in the first period of European contact as when the tribes and the French and English were equal trading partners in the fur industry, beginning in the 1500s)

- European settlement (in the period when the Wampanoag allowed the Pilgrims to settle into the eastern seaboard)

- Treaties, or negotiations made between nations to exchange land, goods, and resources (a strategy that began in the late 1700s to move and take Native lands for the U.S. government)

- Reservations, or defined parcels of land where Native nations were contained (beginning in the late 1800s as a strategy to contain Native people and separate them from their traditional way of life, such as sugaring in their maple forests)

- Public domain, or the U.S. government setting aside land for shared use, such as railroads, the military, timber lands, and mineral lands (a century-plus-old strategy that continues to be used today whenever new resources are found)

- Removal, or ordering Native nations to leave both indigenous tribal lands and reservations (such as when the Ho-Chunk were removed from Wisconsin to Minnesota)

- Allotment, or transferring group-held land to individual Indians, which decimated the land base within reservations (which has resulted in forced land sales leading to "checkerboards" of Native and non-Native holdings within reservation boundaries like White Earth)

- Termination, or closing reservations and removing federal recognition of tribes (a strategy that hasn't disappeared and that is designed to destroy tribal sovereignty: it is very difficult for tribes to survive without their nation-to-nation sovereign status with the U.S. government)

- Relocation, or mid–twentieth century federal policies and assimilation programs designed to lure Native families away from the poverty on the reservations into American cities (such as the Indian Relocation Act of the 1950s)

This list is overwhelming, yet it's just the outer layer of strategic land theft. Have a closer look at any one of these land removal strategies and one discovers hidden treasure chests of deceit.

Take the treaties, for example.

Treaties are legally binding agreements made between nations, the "supreme law of the land," according to the U.S. Constitution. The U.S. government negotiated 367 treaties with Indian tribes between 1778, when the first treaty was signed with the Delaware, and 1868, when the last treaty was signed with the Nez Perce. At least forty-one of these treaties claimed the land called Minnesota. Which treaties, I wondered, were signed to create the 160-acre homestead for my family in The Maples? What is the true story of my ancestors' new home?

※▲▼▲※

To find this story, I began looking at the Minnesota History Center in 1997, but with little success. Back then, treaty records were not held there. Fortunately, that has changed and today much information is available both online and at the History Center in St. Paul. But I didn't find the treaties until a colleague at the Indian Land Tenure Foundation told me about the University of Oklahoma's online database of U.S. treaties. There I was able to read the full transcripts of the government-to-government treaties negotiated to create the 160 acres of land that my great-great-grandparents claimed in The Maples:

  1825   Treaty with the Dakota and Ojibwe
  1837   Treaties with the Dakota and with the Ojibwe
  1846   Treaty with the Ho-Chunk
  1847   Treaties with the Mississippi and Superior
         Ojibwe Bands and with the Pillager Ojibwe
         Band
  1851   Treaties with the Dakota and with the Ojibwe
  1855   Treaties with the Ojibwe Bands

Each treaty took away a significant piece of land from the tribes in Minnesota. Each reduced Native access to their traditional lands and, at the same time, increased the land for European settlers like the Meaghers. Just like any good story, these treaties don't just contain facts and figures. They also contain values and assumptions. At the heart of all of the American treaties with sovereign indigenous nations is a central concept within the European worldview: land can be divided, bought, and sold. Treaties are the Doctrine of Discovery at work on American soil.

The 1825 treaty created a fictitious north-south boundary line to separate the tribes, a boundary that runs along the Watab River a mile from the Meagher homestead land. During these negotiations, Ho-Chunk Chief Caramonee vehemently disagreed with this concept of land ownership when he said: "The lands I claim are mine and the nations here know it is not only claimed by us but by our Brothers. . . . They have held it in common. It would be difficult to divide it. It belongs as much to one as to the other. . . . My Fathers, I do not know that any of my relations had any particular lands." Not only did treaties contradict central indigenous values; the U.S. government did not and has not fully honored the treaties. While our government got the land, the Native tribes did not receive payments due. This happened all across the country, and it happened to make the homestead land the Meaghers claimed accessible to immigrant families like ours.

Take, for example, the 1837 treaty with the Dakota, the original people of Minnesota, in which they ceded all of their lands east of the Mississippi River. In return, the United States agreed to two payments, standard practice for most treaties. There was an immediate cash payout and a deferred payment of interest off of an agreed amount of principal; in this treaty the United States and the Dakota agreed to an immediate cash payout of $4,000. However, traders received $4,000 for horses, goods, and construction of an agency and blacksmith shop. The net amount received by the Dakota, ancestors of the Thanksgiving Pow-Wow emcee Dave Larsen, in their homeland? Zero.

The U.S.–Dakota treaties of 1837 also called for setting aside $300,000 in principal and paying the Dakota at least 5 percent interest per year in perpetuity. Forever. Imagine what the payouts would be today, 125 years later. Yet the Dakota do not receive annual investment income from the U.S. government. All U.S.–Dakota treaties were abrogated after 1862.

The Ojibwe, including the ancestors of Herb and Patty Sam, did not fare much better in 1837. They too have billions of dollars owed to them in unpaid annual investment income. Even the immediate cash payout was dishonorable. The Ojibwe did receive $9,500 in cash once the treaty was signed in 1837. But the traders—many of whom were also working for the government—received $70,000 that day, almost ten times the amount of cash the Ojibwe received for their land.

In the 1846 treaty with the Ho-Chunk, the tribal leaders agreed to leave their Wisconsin homelands in exchange for 800,000 acres in Minnesota, almost 2 percent of the state's current land mass. For several years the Ho-Chunk, including perhaps relatives of Shawnee, the arena director for the Thanksgiving Celebration Pow-Wow, were contained in a reservation near The Maples. When annuity payments were paid, the traders stepped in again. During a Ho-Chunk annuity payout near The Maples, one eyewitness report said:

Opposite Watab on the west side was a beautiful piece of open land known as Watab prairie. Here the Ho-Chunk (Winnebagoes) assembled at times to meet the agent of the tribe and receive their annual payments. For days and weeks they would slowly gather, anticipating the great day. The heads of all families were present, as well as all who were entitled to receive payment in their own right. All around were the teepees of the Indians. There was feasting, frolic, dancing, drumming, granting, parleying, and all sorts of performances. . . . It was my privilege to visit this great camp frequently. I sat in their councils and heard their fiery eloquence. . . . On a large table was spread the records containing the names of each Indian entitled to a money payment and the sum due. As the names were called by the interpreter, each approached the table and the amount of his money was counted out on the table in gold and silver. . . . The recipient signed his name in characters as a receipt but often did not receive any money at all. For close by stood the Indian trader who had financed during the long cold winter previous, with his books of account, and before the Indian could touch a center of money he had to settle with the trader and square his account. . . . Occasionally a brave would try to hold out on him and grab the money, but he was seized, his hand or bag torn open and the right amount subtracted. Away he would then amble, crestfallen, sullen, and disgraced. That Indian would have a hard time getting credit for needed things the next year.

By 1851, both the Dakota and Ojibwe were forced to sign treaties that gave away almost all their remaining lands in Minnesota. The Native tribes had come to realize that the trust agreements would likely not be kept by the U.S. government. As Dakota Chief Wakota said during the 1851 negotiations in Mendota:

> Fathers, your counsel and advice is very good to Indians, but there are a great many different minds and opinions and it appears almost impossible to get an agreement, though we have all been consulting so many days.
>
> Fathers, you have come with the words of our Great Father and have them put in this paper, but the Indians are afraid it may be changed hereafter. I say this in good feeling. Perhaps you may think many of these things will be altered at Washington yourselves! You have been asked a great many questions and have answered yes to them. If all proves as you say it will be very good. But when we were at Washington we were told many things, which when we came back here and attempted to carry them out, we found it could not be done. At the end of three or four years, the Indians found out very different from what they had been told and all were ashamed.
>
> I hope when the people sign this treaty, you will take and deliver it to the President as it is. I want you to write first that I wish the country for our home to be reserved north of where I now live. I was not brought up in a prairie country, but among woods; and I would like to go to a tract of land called Pine Island, which is a good place for Indians. I want you to write this in the treaty. I mention to you my wishes in this respect, but if you do not think it can be complied with and is not right and just, I will say no more about it.

After the 1851 treaty went through, the Dakota, including the ancestors of Thanksgiving Pow-Wow emcee Dave Larsen, were removed to a reservation in the southwestern part of the state—prairie lands—along the Minnesota River, not back to the woods that Wakota longed for. And just as Wakota predicted, the U.S. officials would later change their minds about this prairie reservation.

In 1854, the Dakota reservation was cut in half, forcing all the Dakota of Minnesota to a narrow strip along the southern half of the river without maple sugar stands. In 1861, while Henry David Thoreau was in Minnesota searching for the wild crab apple, he came across an advertisement in the local newspaper advertising a tourist trip up the Minnesota River to observe the annuity payment at the Lower Sioux Agency on this tiny Dakota reservation. The flyer, which I found in Corinne Hosfeld Smith's book *Westward I Go Free: Tracing Thoreau's Last Journey*, read:

GRAND PLEASURE EXCURSION
To the Sioux Agency
The two Steamers,
Frankee Steele, Capt Hatcher,
Favorite, Capt. Bell
of Davidson's Line will make an excursion trip to the
LOWER SIOUX AGENCY
On Monday the 17th day of June
leaving St Paul at 4 PM
and arriving at the agency in time to
Witness the Payments
Which will come off on the 19th and 20th.
This will afford a good opportunity to persons wishing to visit this
SPLENDID REGION OF COUNTRY
And of witnessing the ceremonies of payment of nearly
FIVE THOUSAND INDIANS.

Hardly a tourist destination, the reservation contained Dakota families who were struggling to survive on the harsh windy prairie lands and far from the central hardwoods and maple groves they once called home. When Thoreau and the traveling steamboats arrived in Redwood and the Lower Sioux Agency where the annuity payouts were to take place, he noted in his journal that the Indians looked "hungry, not sleek and round-faced."

Once the annuity payment process got under way, another viewer reported that Mdewakanton spokesman Red Owl's "complaints were many and bitter. Said they had been promised all these things before, and had been cheated out of them," and that the Indians never got "more than enough to cover the nakedness of their women and children," and that the Indian agent had mismanaged funds, requesting that the Dakota be given "a store-house of their own where the goods cannot slip through any body's fingers," or their allocations "scattered about the State, or carted off to another tribe to be returned in small parcels or not at all."

The annuity payout of food and cash originally scheduled for June 19 didn't happen at Lower Sioux until a week later, on June 26. Upper Sioux families didn't receive their payment of cash and food for another week where another witness reported the traders theft of the Dakota payments, just as the Ho-Chunk experienced on the Watab near The Maples. This witness writes: "Many Indian pay before the payment with furs[;] still they are caught up by these Traders, and very seldom a man passes away with his money. I saw a poor fellow one day swallow his money. I wondered he did not choke to death, but he said, 'They will not have mine, for I do not owe them.'"

Thoreau summed up the situation in his journal, recording that the Dakota had "the advantage in point of truth and earnestness, and therefore of eloquence. . . . They were quite dissatisfied with the white man's treatment of them and probably have reason to be so." Then he boarded the steamer and headed back up the Minnesota River and returned home to Massachusetts.

Within a year's time the Dakota went to war: the U.S.–Dakota War of 1862.

There wasn't agreement even among the Dakota, but eventually they decided to assert the integrity of their sovereignty in their homeland, not so different from the American rebels on the Battle Green in Lexington. They decided to go to war because their children were hungry. Not unlike my Potato Famine ancestors.

During this six-week war up at The Maples, the pioneers braced themselves for attack. A local history reports:

> Most of the men from the settlement were called to Fort
> Ripley, but a few stayed back to protect their properties.
> They, the women and the children gathered at the Demerrit
> house, the largest one in the neighborhood. There they
> passed the anxious days, scarcely daring to cook for fear the
> smoke would betray them, or to have a light at night lest
> it might attract the attention of the Indians. Many buried
> their few valuables in the fields or woods that they might
> be saved in case the houses were burned by the Indians.

I remember my father quizzing me about the war. He seemed almost as frightened as the Irish in The Maples. "Didn't they rape our women?" he asked, repeating something he'd learned in Minnesota history as a child. No, I explained. Tragic losses occurred on both sides, but the only rapes I had found in my research were those perpetrated against Dakota women. Yet for generations Minnesotans have neither learned about nor acknowledged the U.S. atrocities against the Dakota. They learned lies.

It took just six weeks for U.S. and Minnesota troops to force a Dakota surrender. Yet after forced marches from the Dakota reservation to Fort Snelling and the hangings on the day after Christmas in Mankato—the largest mass execution in U.S. history—the U.S. attack on the Dakota continued. Our governor, Alexander Ramsey, said, "The Sioux Indians of Minnesota must be exterminated or driven forever beyond the borders of the state."

The state offered $200 bounties for each dead Dakota. Families, like Charles Eastman's, fled out of their homeland and the maple groves, across the Dakotas and up into Canada. Those who didn't escape were imprisoned or loaded up onto boats and sent to reservations in South Dakota and Nebraska. Perhaps to celebrate the state's victory, the Minnesota Historical Society displayed the head of one Dakota leader for decades, not unlike the fate of the Wampanoag leader Philip in Massachusetts. Though the museum display is long gone, an 1863 federal law forbidding the Dakota from entering their beloved homeland remains on the books today.

In the same year as the U.S.–Dakota War, 1862, the U.S. Homestead Act passed in Congress. My great-great-grandparents were allowed to legally claim the 160 acres they had squatted on in The Maples since 1858. Ownership of 160 acres was made possible through the Homestead Act, a new chapter of U.S. strategies designed to take indigenous lands. Within their township, free land was also granted to veterans, to the railroads, and to the state for the education of its citizens. "Free" land or next-to-free land for hardworking people and companies with roots in Europe or New England.

Non-Native friends and colleagues sometimes argue that my Irish ancestors were not directly culpable for what happened to the Ojibwe, Dakota, and Ho-Chunk. Sure, we weren't government officials, designing or enforcing the policies that led to land theft. We were hungry farmers, victims of the Potato Famine. We weren't treaty negotiators or signers. But we signed the papers that gave us 160 acres in The Maples. We weren't traders. But we freely took those 160 acres in The Maples—at dear cost to the Ojibwe, the Ho-Chunk, and above all the Dakota.

As I try to shed the lens of dominion, I can finally begin to hear these true stories. Not Laura's story, not Paul's story, not our Thanksgiving myth. I am finally reading the whole story here in The Maples, a forest that was cleared of its trees and its people—the Dakota, the Ojibwe, and the Ho-Chunk—by the Meaghers and my aproned great-great-grandmother Katie. This is my family's Doctrine of Discovery.

Wild Rice

THE CABIN IN THE MAPLES HAD JUST ONE WINDOW, adorned with a ledge where my great-great-grandmother used to set pies to cool. Though late-summer rains and winter winds were no stranger to the one-room house, little sunlight made it through the oilcloth stretched across the modest window frame. For my great-great-grandparents, this cabin and their 160-acre parcel was home. Was it any rougher than the damp cottage they had left behind in Ireland? Likely not. The winters were colder for sure, but on homestead land in The Maples the Meaghers didn't have to give up a portion of their potatoes and a cash tip to the landlord each year. The government in this new land had told them that the land and the crops they grew were theirs for keeps.

Hewn from the felled maples, cracks filled with mottled clay, the cabin contained only three pieces of furniture—a large rough table, a cookstove, and a long bench along one wall. Even so, the cabin signaled ownership. Did Katie Hughes and John Meagher realize they were the new landlords? Did they ever meet their "colonial subjects"—the Dakota, Ojibwe, and Ho-Chunk—whose land they had taken?

Our official documents, even if they are somewhat fictional like the treaties, sketch the outline of dominion. They don't report impact. When the Meaghers were tucked into their one-room cabin at night in The Maples, what was happening inside the lodges of our Native hosts? I call on one storyteller in my family. My great-grandmother—daughter of Katie Hughes, mother of my grandfather the judge.

Mary was born in 1861 in the tiny Meagher cabin in The Maples one year before the U.S.–Dakota War and one hundred years before me. It's said that she met her husband while working in a boardinghouse serving food to working men. He was an Irish stonecutter from Boston who'd migrated west in search of work in the central Minnesota granite quarries. Stone he later fashioned into the Cathedral of St. Paul. After they married, they moved to St. Cloud, a river town just south of The Maples. It was in St. Cloud where my grandfather Murphy and his eight siblings were born and raised.

My father's first memory was of sitting on his grandmother Mary's lap as she swung back and forth in a glider on their back porch overlooking the Mississippi River in St. Cloud. Mary died before my father was old enough to remember the words she shared with him. He carried only the feeling of safety. But my father's older sister remembers, and I am grateful she passed them on to me. "There were still a few Indians around The Maples when I was growing up," my great-grandmother Mary Meagher Murphy had told my aunt. "One day my sister and I were alone in the cabin," she would have continued.

It is hard to conceive of this pioneer girl at home all alone with just one sibling. There were eight children;

six of them were girls. Ten to the single-room cabin. Where had everyone else gone on the day that Mary recalled? To work in the fields? Help build a barn at a neighbor's? Wake a fellow Tipperarian who hadn't made it through the winter? There is no answer. We only know that on this day the girls were alone. Six and eight years old, perhaps, already trained in the daily chores of a pioneer woman: milking, tending to the fire, mending, stirring stew in the big black pot.

"We heard something or someone approaching the cabin, so we looked out the oilcloth window and saw a shadow," Mary might have added.

"My sister grabbed my hand when we heard someone or something tugging at the rusty iron latch at the front door. We snuck into the narrow spot between the cabin walls and the straw mattress on the floor and crouched down low. My heart was beating so fast, as I hadn't any idea what would be coming in through the front door. A bear? A priest?

"Next thing you know it, in walk two Indian men. Right into our cabin. I wanted to scream, but my sister clasped her hand over my mouth to prevent me from making a sound. So we stayed in our corner, completely still, completely silent as we watched the two men."

With just one window, decorated with a pie ledge and covered in dim oilcloth, the two Native men who came visiting the Meagher cabin that day wouldn't have been able to look in and know for certain if anyone was home. They would have opened the door and walked in.

"They didn't stay long, but before they left the two Indians tried on our parents' hats," my great-grandmother said. The pioneers of Minnesota wore plenty of hats—cotton bonnets and starched brimmed hats with feathers, low riders with brims and stovepipe hats like chimneys. But Ojibwe scholar Rebecca Kugel explained to me that her ancestors did not traditionally wear hats until after contact with Europeans. A somewhat affectionate term for Europeans in the Ojibwe language means "those who wear hats."

Who were these two Native men who tried on hats in the Meagher cabin that day? Were they strangers to Mary and her sister? Or men known to them in The Maples? Our family story doesn't say. One thing is for certain: it's possible the men were relatives of my friends at the Minneapolis Thanksgiving Pow-Wow. Let's do the math.

The year of the hat story in The Maples would have been about 1868. That's after the U.S.–Dakota War of 1862 and after the exile that forced the Dakota out of their homeland here in Minnesota. So the visitors were probably not the ancestors of Dave Larsen, the Thanksgiving Pow-Wow emcee. The year 1863 saw the removal of the Ho-Chunk. That means the visitors weren't likely relatives of the powwow arena director, Shawnee Hunt, either.

Post-1862 for the Ojibwe brought a slashing in the number of reservations in the northern half of the state. Patty Sam's family was probably removed to the Lac Courte Oreilles Reservation over in Wisconsin by then. That leaves Herb. Some of Herb's family had been forced to a new reservation called White Earth after 1862. Yet others had remained at Mille Lacs, defending their home on this rich lake filled with walleye and wild rice. Defending their right to hunt and tap sugar in The Maples.

The men in the Meagher cabin could have been relatives of Herb Sam.

꘏꘏꘏

My great-grandmother Mary's second story has to do with food, not hats.

Though this one likely involved the Ojibwe in The Maples, food had become scarce for all tribes in Minnesota after my ancestors arrived. Cut off from their lands, the tribes had very limited or no access to their traditional foods. Foods like wild rice. *Psin* in Dakota, or *manoomin*, as it is known in Ojibwe. Both nations relied on the annual rice harvest for survival. Wild rice was the promised food that grows in water in the prophecy that led the Ojibwe to journey from the East Coast inland to Lake Superior five hundred years ago. The Dakota had harvested wild rice long before that: ruins from ancient village sites around Mille Lacs show proof.

Six months after the maple trees offer the people their sap, wild rice ripens, ready for harvest in late summer and early fall. But for indigenous people, I have been taught, food is more than just needed calories and nutrition. *Wild Rice White Paper*, written by a coalition of Ojibwe nations, also known as the Anishinaabeg, in 2010, explains the deep and complex network of relationships their nation has with the rice:

> *Manoomin is a living entity that has its own unique spirit. Anishinaabeg have a responsibility to respect that spirit and to care for it. Anishinaabe people depended on the wild rice harvest prior to and throughout the treaty and reservation eras, and continue to view themselves as caretakers*

of wild rice in its unique ecosystem. Twentieth century
scholars have maintained that the entire indigenous legal
system designed by the Anishinaabe was for the purpose of
protecting wild rice in its habitat, noting that "what serves
the rice is law; what harms the rice is illegal."

In three of the treaties that formed Minnesota's land
base, the Ojibwe had negotiated for the right to gather
wild rice throughout their northern Minnesota lands in
perpetuity. In the late twentieth century this right was
challenged by non-Native folks. Protests in the 1980s
and 1990s up at Mille Lacs were extremely violent,
deadly for Native people. But in 1999, the U.S. Supreme
Court upheld Ojibwe ricing rights. Threats continue
however—through agriculture and research.

Rice in Minnesota also calls to mind Henry Rice.
Those of us schooled here know him as one of the early
great statesmen, though we may not remember exactly what Henry did. Nevertheless, we keep his memory
alive through place names. We have a Rice County, a
Rice Street, dozens of Rice Lakes, and many Rice Parks.

The Rice Park I know best is the one in downtown
St. Paul. This charming square is our most elegant outdoor gathering place. It features trees, winding paths,
and a circular pool. In the summer, musicians play live
music over the lunch hour. In winter, Christmas lights
illuminate a small skating rink and an ice sculpture con-
test. A bronze sculpture of an Indian maiden, created
by Paul Manship, stands alone in a circular pool in Rice
Park all year long. Entrapped inside the pool, the Indian
maiden is frozen in time, isolated, and contained like
an extinct animal.

So how did Henry Rice earn so many place names

in Minnesota? To host a regal park with a trapped Indian maiden?

Our Henry Rice was born in Vermont to a family with English roots and ties to the Massachusetts Bay Colony. Henry swapped life in New England to work in the fur trade in the Midwest. In his work as a profitable trader, Henry developed a specialty in negotiating with the Ho-Chunk and the Ojibwe. Later he became one of the first senators of Minnesota—a position he held during the 1862 U.S.–Dakota War.

His story and my family's story intersect in 1847. Henry negotiated three treaties that year with the Ojibwe, including the one with the Pillager Band that included the exact 160-acre homestead Katie Hughes and John Meagher claimed in The Maples. The land where they built their small cabin, gave birth to my great-grandmother Mary the storyteller, and where she and her sister met two Indians who tried on their parents' hats.

By 1847, the United States had already established a paper trail of treaties claiming all the land east of the Mississippi River. Next, it eyed Ojibwe lands on the west side of the river. The U.S. government identified a chunk of land in central Minnesota that was west of the river and north of that 1825 Dakota–Ojibwe divide— that imaginary borderline separating the Dakota and the Ojibwe that ran just a few miles south of The Maples. To get this western tract of land, the United States tapped Henry Rice to help them negotiate a treaty with at least two federations of Ojibwe—the Mississippi and the Superior Bands. The family of Herb Sam belonged to the Mississippi Band. Patty Sam's belonged to the Superior Band.

The negotiations for this triangular chunk of land west of the Mississippi with both bands took place at Fond du Lac near the southern tip of Lake Superior. Neither band believed they were selling the actual land to the U.S. government. During oral negotiations, the Ojibwe agreed only to *lease* the land, not *sell* the central hardwood land in question.

The signers of this dual 1847 treaty included Ojibwe Chief Hole in the Day; William Warren, a mixed European Ojibwe whose father and father-in-law were fur traders; dozens of Ojibwe men representing the federation of Mississippi and Superior Bands; and five European American traders and businessmen, including Henry Rice.

An unusual feature of the 1847 treaty was that it provided different payments for the two bands. Both were promised a lump payment of $17,000. Yet the Mississippi Band, including Herb's at Mille Lacs, was to be paid an additional $46,000 in $1,000 annual payments for the next forty-six years. Patty Sam's band didn't receive anything above the initial $17,000. According to Don Wedll, the tribal historian up at Mille Lacs, the Superior Band members weren't too happy with the Mississippi Band once they found out about the additional payments.

Now, remember, Henry Rice also had a day job: he was a fur trader and was in the business of selling and trading goods. The added benefit of being a treaty negotiator was that traders like Henry could line their pockets with revenue from the sales of goods often tacked onto the end of the treaties, as shown during the annuity payouts for the Ho-Chunk and the Dakota. Henry hadn't sold any goods to the Mississippi and Superior

Bands of Ojibwe in the dual 1847 treaty negotiations at Fond du Lac, so this entrepreneur hatched a plan.

Here's what historian Bruce White told me happened next. The U.S. government had eyed a second parcel of land immediately west of the chunk that the Superior and Mississippi Bands had just leased, or sold, depending on whom you talked to. This adjacent parcel was where a third band of Ojibwe, the Pillager Band, lived. Henry Rice didn't want any other traders present at a treaty with the Pillagers for this western chunk. If other traders were there, he would have to share any profit.

To cut out the competition, he told everyone that he would not pursue the Pillager treaty. Then as he left Fond du Lac in early August, he first headed east in the direction opposite of the Pillager Band trading post. The other European and American negotiators and traders followed Henry's lead and also headed east and then south, back to Fort Snelling in the Twin Cities. But once Henry got far enough east to lose some of the fellow traders and negotiators, he secretly cut west and sneaked back west over to Leech Lake. There he negotiated the third 1847 treaty with the Pillager Band of Ojibwe, minus one U.S. commissioner and other traders. In this third treaty, Rice secured for the Pillagers the most detailed list of goods that appears in any Minnesota treaty. Article 4 of the 1847 Pillager treaty states:

> *The U.S. agrees to furnish the Pillager band of Indians annually for five years, the following articles:*
>
> > *50 3-pt Mackinaw new blankets*
> > *300 2.5-pt Mackinaw new blankets*
> > *50 1.5-pt Mackinaw new blankets*

340 yards of gray list cloth

450 yards of white list scarlet cloth

1800 yards of strong dark prints, assorted colors

150 pounds three-thread gray gilly-twine

75 pounds turtle twine

50 bunches sturgeon twine

25 pounds linen thread

200 combs

5000 assorted needles

150 medal-looking glasses

10 pounds vermillion

30 nests (14 each) heavy tiny kettles

500 pounds tobacco

5 barrels salt

The U.S. also agreed to give as a present, 200 warranted beaver traps and 75 northwest guns.

But without land, how long would these goods be useful to the Pillagers? Not long. The conqueror's plenty would leave the Ojibwe hungry.

Father Pierz, the Catholic priest from Europe who once called for his compatriots to settle land around The Maples, catalogued the growing hunger of the Ojibwe near his mission in letters. He expressed increasing distress over the conditions his parishes were facing. In one letter to his superior, Pierz wrote, "At present season in which the game is not so plenty, they are reduced to great poverty and want." With diminished land and little access to their traditional sources of food—game, maple sugar, fish, and the sacred manoomin—the tribes in Minnesota became dependent on food annuities agreed on in the treaty negotiations. But the annuity food payments at the trading posts were not always dependable or safe. In an 1854 letter, Father Pierz describes the abysmal foods given at the payouts:

> *Three years ago [1851] after the payment was made, the Chippeways of Sandy Lake received such bad flour, that on their way home 400 died of Colic. The Indians said that the dough looked like potter's clay. I suppose the flour having been strongly mixed with white magnesia clay, which I had seen in Ohio in considerable quantity, for I myself found a year ago a considerable portion of this poisonous clay in the flour, given to the Indians.*

Flour laced with potter's clay that poisoned and killed the bands of Herb and Patty wasn't the only danger in the food given to the Ojibwe in central Minnesota. Father Pierz continued:

> *There is still another disadvantage for the Indians, causes derived from the annual payment they receive. It is on account of the well polished copper kettles, in which they cook victuals without being aware that these kettles contain a poisonous copperas. What makes it still worse is that these kettles are hardly ever washed and that the Indians fill them up with meat, which left in them for two or three days and thus gets poisoned by copperas. The Indians then eat often times the whole of it at once, after which they die away like flies without knowing any cause at all. I saw very often with my own eyes sick and dying persons, whose symptoms and color indicated that they had been poisoned in said manner.*

The Ojibwe in the northern half of the state weren't the only Native tribe hungry and dying in Minnesota by the time the Meaghers transformed the maple grove into a land of plenty for themselves. In 1851, four years after the three 1847 Ojibwe treaties, Henry Rice received $10,000 from fellow fur traders to get the Dakota signatures needed to wrest the entire southern half of Minnesota away from Dakota hands—the largest exchange of land in the state. Henry succeeded, though no one knows how. Several Dakota colleagues of mine say that alcohol was involved—not at the treaty table but with government assistance in the nearby town.

It was hunger that started the U.S.–Dakota War.

By 1854, the Dakota had been removed to one narrow strip along the southern side of the Minnesota River in the southwestern Minnesota prairies. As Henry David Thoreau noted on his visit in 1861, the Dakota on the paltry Minnesota River reservation were starving that year. But Andrew Myrick, the Indian agent at Lower Sioux, refused to release the annuity food payments he had locked up in the agency storehouse. He was awaiting the accompanying cash payment from Washington. "Let them eat grass" was his retort.

It took the U.S. government just six weeks to force a Dakota surrender in the battle that followed. After the war, the Dakota endured forced marches, the December 26 mass execution, imprisonment, rape, and exile from their homeland. Families that escaped being loaded onto boats down the Minnesota to the Missouri River and the Crow Creek Reservation in South Dakota fled farther west. Many made it to safety in Canada, Montana, and North Dakota. But the U.S. Calvary hounded these fleeing Dakota families, bringing those they captured into prisons, like Camp McClellan in Iowa, where

265 Dakota men were chained and shackled. Hunger followed the Dakota everywhere. More than a thousand women and children died of starvation their first year at Crow Creek.

After the Dakota men at Camp McClellan were released from their shackles, they were forced to work on nearby farms. Joining them in 1864 were ninety men, women, and children who had been picked up by the U.S. Calvary and were imprisoned with the men in Iowa. With the help of missionaries, these men and women wrote letters that were translated and published by two Dakota scholars—Clifford Canku and Michael Simons—only in 2013. The prisoners' letters tell of so much suffering and hunger. "We are living in great difficulty with little or no food, therefore I want you to pursue getting us plenty of food to eat—it is so," wrote a man named Caske, or First Born Son, in 1864. A man named Wasteste wrote: "I just received word from the Missouri River [Crow Creek]. The people are starving this winter, there they are starving from starvation. This saddens me very much, much relative."

Stands on Earth Woman wrote: "I want you to help me because of the infant, so the other can live, both of us should not depend on you. I am suffering for the lack of food and clothing. If you can give me back my money, I will thank you. I need shoes and something to eat. I am suffering very much, I came home, but then they said my husband died long ago."

⸙⸙⸙

Meanwhile, we pioneers grew fat off the land. Sure, the Potato Famine immigrants struggled at first, especially after several years of locusts. But in 1880, the farmers in The Maples produced 17,654 bushels of wheat; 16,168 bushels of oats; 4,285 bushels of corn; 2,891 bushels of potatoes; as well as some rye, barley, and hay. They also produced 863 pounds of wool, 8,012 pounds of butter, and 3 pounds of honey. Imagine the flaky buttery breads and pies that young Mary or Bridget or their mother, Katie Hughes Meagher, could have made with all this gold. They did.

Recall that my great-grandmother Mary passed along two stories about the Indians in The Maples. One about hats and a second story about food.

"And another time," Mary would have continued telling her grandchildren on the wooded porch above the Mississippi River in St. Cloud. "The Indians came and stole the pies cooling on the window ledge at our cabin."

Stole?

"You see, when we were little, mother always used to put the pies she baked in the old cookstove out on the window ledge to cool. Sometimes she would turn around only to find that the pies had disappeared from the ledge."

The thief left only one clue: the swish of the bushes at the edge of the clearing where the Meagher cabin stood.

Often our American story ends there. Think only of the ugly term *Indian giver*.

But my great-grandmother Mary's story continued: "A few days later, we'd come home to find that the Indians had come by and set fresh game on the front step."

White Birch

T HE FIRST DAYS OF WINTER BRING TEMPERATURES that alternate between below zero and warm spells. The crab apple doesn't seem to mind the chaos. She stands resolute in her old-lady form, a reminder to the rest of us all that things do change. An eight-inch snowstorm arrives. Soon after, the temperatures rise back up into the fifties, giving the city workers time to return and dig up the elm stump on the boulevard out front. But before you know it, the snow is here to stay.

Winter in Minnesota stretches from November all the way through the beginning of April. It's cold and dark for so long that we can completely forget what lilacs look like. We forget the sound of a robin calling its mate or the smell of a soft rain in an evening whose light tumbles toward midnight. Light and dark, warm and cold, these two faces of our northern landscape fix the mind like an optical illusion.

Recall the famous optical illusion of two ladies. One of the ladies is old and withered, not unlike my crab apple tree. She sports an ugly wrinkle on her nose. The other lady is young and beautiful. She wears a fashionable hat and necklace. When you first look at this illusion, only one of the two ladies comes to view. Seeing the second lady requires you to consciously reorganize the visual clues in the image. It's almost impossible to see both ladies at the same time. That's because it's difficult for the brain to gather visual information that tells two competing stories. It's difficult to give up old patterns of thinking.

How we understand our nation, our people, and this land also depends on how we organize information. Our minds can get trapped into seeing things just one way. Like believing that this land freely belongs to the descendants of the English colonists and their European progeny. Descendants like Laura and Paul in the big woods. Like my family in The Maples.

We see the land as ours. Our manifest destiny. We don't want to let this first image go.

Yet there is another, older story in America. Rearrange the clues and the second lady—the story of American Indians and the devastating losses they endured yet survived—comes into view. The story of the Doctrine of Discovery. The story of Thanksgiving in Massachusetts. The story of the treaties in Minnesota. The ghastly story of hunger and war. The story of giving thanks in The Maples for a pie on a cabin window ledge.

Until we can see these American stories, we remain ignorant of our true history and our relationship to this land. To do so requires letting go of both what we learned and how we learned to see this land and its people.

○●○●○

In winter, there's one tree that can be hard to see. The white birch. Its white papery bark blends in with the snow that surrounds it. In Minnesota, the birch grows in the central hardwoods and the northern forests, a companion to both the maples and the pines. Birch has been a friend to Native people in Minnesota for thousands of years. From writing on birch bark scrolls to traveling in birch bark canoes along our lakes and rivers, humans have long benefited from the gifts of this tree. Long before copper or iron kettles were traded for furs, the first people of Minnesota boiled sap during the sugaring season in The Maples in birch baskets. Though we no longer journey in birch canoes, inscribe our history on birch scrolls, or boil down sweet sap in birch buckets, this tree still fills our woods and makes excellent kindling for fires.

Humans have told stories across time and place by the fire. But what happens if we have been taught the wrong story? What if we were taught not to tell our true stories? In this winter season, perhaps the last with my dying crab apple, I light a fire with birch kindling. In its flickering light, I vow to make out why these camouflaged American myths have persisted.

Education—what we get told and not told as children—is the kindling for our deceit.

My formal study of history began in third grade in a classroom in the shadow of Tower Hill, guardian of our hilly neighborhood across the river from where the Minneapolis American Indian Center sits today. Our teacher, Mrs. Brennan, handed us Popsicle sticks and cream-colored construction paper she'd shredded to mimic birch bark. Then we went outside and across the street to Tower Hill to gather twigs and grasses. Back in the classroom, we settled in for a week of building miniature wigwams. The homes of the Indians who used to live here.

Next, we spent an entire morning taking turns shaking a sealed bottle of cream. By lunchtime, the liquid had turned solid. We used plastic knives to spread our homemade butter on rolls at our wooden desks. Though I don't think our teacher ever explicitly said anything, the implicit hierarchy was clear. The Ojibwe who had lived in wigwams were dead, like brittle twigs and dried grasses. We were meant to draw our strength from the white pioneers and their buttered bread.

Fourth grade reaffirmed this hierarchy. We learned about the British and the Americans fighting for independence. We learned about the 1803 Louisiana Purchase from France, which brought present-day Minnesota into our nation. We learned about Henry Sibley and Alexander Ramsey and Henry Rice. We learned about the state flower and the state bird. We took a field trip to the State Capitol, where my grandfather Murphy worked as a judge. There the tour guide showed us the Minnesota state flag flying in one of the legislative chambers. The flag depicts a White farmer plowing land and an American Indian man on horseback riding west off into the horizon. Then we swallowed this pioneer–Indian hierarchy once again when we read *Little House in the Big Woods*. I reaffirmed it every summer rereading the Paul Bunyan book at my grandparents' farm on the prairie. Thirty years later, my children relearn it in their classrooms, too.

There is a price for seeing just one side of the story.

Those of us who look like the good guys remain trapped behind walls of fear, indifference, and hatred.

This was the fear I encountered in my own heart the day I started working at the Indian Center, the indifference I had learned as a child growing up on Tower Hill, and the hatred I learned in our nation's stories.

There is also a price for those whom the story demonizes or ignores.

Native people living near the historic Lower Sioux Agency that Thoreau visited in 1861 still experience racism today. For instance, every year during November—nationally designated as American Indian month—Dakota students endure overt and covert threats from their White peers at school.

In 150 years, so little has changed. Wedded to our stories of dominion, our nation and our schools still harm our Native students. Our schools continue to teach our history through a European and European American lens. Is it any surprise that Native students have the lowest high school graduation rates in the state? That Minnesota Native students have the lowest high school graduation rate in the entire country?

Recall that there were at least eight methods by which the U.S. government took land from the five hundred-plus tribes in this continent, including treaties and reservations, allotment and relocation. However, in addition to land theft, U.S. political leaders also used ten more strategies to force Native assimilation. Two of these additional strategies we've already seen in The Maples: war and restricted access to traditional foods. The U.S. government also intentionally enacted policies to destroy Native self-determination, economy, access to resources, culture, language, religion, and family structure.

Last, education was used as a tenth strategy to conquer indigenous peoples in the United States. When my ancestors arrived from Ireland, they understood what it was like to be taught not to see themselves at school. The English had outlawed schools for Irish children and outlawed the transmission of Irish stories and Irish culture for centuries. This was why Katie Hughes, Katie Aodh of the fire, would never have gone to a proper school. Instead, she climbed up a windy path along the Horse Hill to an outdoor hedge school where the descendant of druids and Brehons, the arbitrators or judges, shared their Irish stories in secret.

Once the Meaghers got to The Maples, they built a second cabin on their homestead land and hired Clara Thorpe, a young woman from New England, to live there and teach the children. A few years later, The Maples opened a larger school in town. Yet while the children in The Maples were getting a formal education, quite the opposite was happening for Native children in Minnesota. In 1819, the U.S. government passed the Indian Civilization Act, which was designed to support Native assimilation action across the country. The government began paying $10,000 chunks to churches, missionaries, and religious groups to educate American Indians out on the American "frontier" like the wild woods of Minnesota. As Father Pierz wrote in 1855 of the Ojibwe in his mission:

> There appears to me to be no other way to remove these pitiful widows and children from the dangers to which they are exposed, than by bringing them into charitable institutions, in which they might receive moral and religious education and along with that be instructed in economy and manual labor according to their sex and condition. . . .

This in my opinion is the right, yea, the only way to promote the common welfare of the Chippeway nation.

But Father Pierz also chronicles the abuses of these
loosely organized schools in Minnesota:

The kind American Government has been anxious during
the past 15 years to take measures in order to advance the
moral and political civilization of these savages. Money
to be spent for said purpose, was put into the hands of
Protestant Ministers, who do not understand the proper
method of instruction for Indians. These Ministers are
more solicitous for their own interests than the welfare
and salvation of the Indians. These Gentlemen come to the
Indians with well laden wagons or boats and by making
some presents to the Indians easily obtain permission to
establish a mission among them. They draw up a long list
of scholars in order to send promising reports both to the
Government and committee. But as soon as the Minister
manifests any earnestness in teaching the English language,
for which the Indian children have a dislike, or if he dis-
continues to support them, scholars will come no more. The
schoolmaster rings the school bell year after year without
having any scholars, yet he gives in an annual school report
to the Government that he may continue to receive his
annual salary. Likewise he reports to the committee of the
mission in order to obtain merchandise and provisions for
the purpose of making presents to the Indians, whilst he
himself is becoming a rich merchant selling goods and provisions, until he is chased away by the Indians or disgusted
goes away willingly to continue the same missionary labor
at some other place.

By the 1880s, perhaps recognizing the inefficiency of
the independent frontier schools, the U.S. government

formalized the Indian reeducation policy by establishing boarding schools, a structural, national system of forced reeducation. These new boarding schools were run both by the government and by Christian and Catholic missionaries. For more than one hundred years Native children were removed from their families—often forcibly—and were punished for speaking their indigenous language or practicing their traditions.

It happened right near The Maples.

Not ten miles from the Meagher homestead, Father Pierz's confreres, the Benedictines, had established monasteries for nuns and monks, St. Ben's and St. John's. Both the nuns and the monks educated Indian children in their monasteries for several years. After these closed, the nuns founded a Catholic mission school on White Earth Reservation in 1878 and later a second Indian school up at Red Lake Reservation. This White Earth school was lucrative—the nuns at St. Ben's received $108 per student per quarter. This meant up to $64,800 in annual earnings between 1891 and 1945, the year the mission school at White Earth closed.

The experience in the boarding school was almost always feared by the families or the tribes. Like the Irish before English conquest, Native communities had their own traditional systems of education that had been passed down for thousands of years. Within the walls of the mission boarding schools, Native students lost access to their indigenous education. The students also faced loss of language, culture, and family. Students were beaten for speaking Dakota or Ojibwe. Students were punished if they offered tobacco to the trees in prayer to the Creator. Students were forced to stay away from their families, causing generational rifts that have been hard to mend. Sometimes the experiences in the boarding schools were so painful that the trauma remains intact, a wound in the heart that is so raw it cannot heal. Native friends have confided that they are unable to talk about what happened to them as children at boarding school.

Inside these government schools and mission schools, generations were forced to give up their spiritual teachings. "White Spider, my father, told me that the Indians had a simple religion—one whereby they lived by nature, having great respect for everything that God had created, such as the sun, the moon, the stars, the trees. The Sioux had the idea of one great spirit who guided man," said the niece of Little Crow, the Dakota chief whose head was displayed at the Minnesota Historical Society for decades.

In describing what it was like to be forced to give up their religion in order to survive the boarding school, Ojibwe journalist Wub-e-ke-niew from Red Lake wrote: "I spent nine years as a political prisoner in boarding schools that White man created. One of the first things they showed me was . . . a picture of a man nailed to a cross, bleeding all over. They said, this is your savior."

American Indian spirituality was illegal in the United States until the 1978 Freedom of Religion Act was passed.

To many the single greatest harm of the boarding school era was the devastation to language. There is a reason we sometimes call our native language the "mother tongue." It is in family, as infants and children, that our mothers teach us to speak. With the gift of these first words, we connect to one another and to the land.

Today, Minnesota has just a hundred fluent Ojibwe

speakers and just five Dakota elders who grew up speaking Dakota in their homeland. In recent years I have had the honor to meet some of these elder speakers in my work with the Native nonprofit Dakota Wicohan. *Wicohan* means Dakota way of life and is pronounced "wee-choh-hahn." This educational organization was founded by an intergenerational group of activists who seek to reconnect the community to their language and traditional lifeways. Though the organization involves Dakota people from around the state, its office is located just a few miles from the Lower Sioux Agency near the banks of the Minnesota River that Henry David Thoreau visited in 1861.

Funding is always a challenge for this organization, which connects two hundred-plus community members of all ages to language and leadership training every year. It was long housed in a dilapidated outbuilding behind the abandoned brick Indian school built in the late 1800s. As soon as it gets cold, the pipes freeze and the language learners have to go for periods without water and plumbing. One winter these hearty students had to use a porta potty set at the entrance to the outbuilding for three months.

Undeterred, Dakota Wicohan completed a documentary in 2013 that features interviews with elder speakers they had collected over five years. Many of these elders have now passed on, so the content within the film and a companion handbook they produced offer extremely precious threads of wisdom and knowledge for the next generation. When asked about boarding schools and their impact on the language, the Dakota elders shared openly about the challenges they experienced as children. "You couldn't talk Indian at school, couldn't talk English at home, and for me it was confusing," explains Dakota elder Garrett Wilson in the documentary.

Gary Cavendar reveals what happened inside the classroom: "One day, the teacher asked me a question. She pressured me to answer her. I forgot my English, so I spoke Dakota. Then she got very angry. 'Come stand here!' she said. I obeyed and stood there. I held out my hand. She had a ruler with a metal edge. 'We don't speak that devil's language here. We speak English.' Then she hit me. She really hurt me."

Lower Sioux community elder LaVonne Swenson explained what happened to the mother tongue in many families: "To protect us, our parents decided not to teach us the language." Yet these elders also teach that the language itself is still strong: it is a gift from the Creator and it cannot die. "This language here is spiritual," said elder Genevieve LaBatte, an elder from Upper Sioux who died a few years ago.

Today the hard work of reconnecting the people to the original languages of this land is under way—not just at Dakota Wicohan but around the state. Herb and Patty send their granddaughter to an Ojibwe language immersion school up at Mille Lacs. Here in the Cities, a new charter school teaching both Dakota and Ojibwe opened recently, named Bdote Learning Center in honor of the sacred origin of the Dakota, the confluence of the Mississippi and Minnesota Rivers.

This work isn't just important for the Dakota and Ojibwe. It is important for all of us.

My colleague Teresa Peterson of Upper Sioux, a co-founder of Dakota Wicohan, explains why: "The language is healing to me and my relationships with my family, extended family, community, and this land. By reclaiming the Dakota language, I feel like I'm returning home." She continues: "The story of the Dakota language is also important for every Minnesotan. If we don't understand what happened to the Dakota and the original language of this land, we can't fully appreciate what it means to be home, here in Minnesota."

Her words force me to rethink the optical illusion we use to see and relate to this land. Can language help us reclaim the truths so many of us have missed—intentionally or unintentionally?

Yes. Even the words we use in our stories matter.

Here's one example. In Dakota, one way to say "earth" is *Kunsi Maka*. *Kunsi* is pronounced with a soft *g* and soft *sh*. The *un* is nasal. It sounds to me like goo-shee. The *ka* in *maka* is pronounced with an elongated soft *a*. The emphasis is on the second syllable in both words. *Kunsi Maka*. What does the Dakota word for earth literally mean in English? *Maka* means the land. *Kunsi* means grandmother. The land of your grandmother.

"How would you treat your grandmother?" a Dakota elder who had been sent to boarding school asked me. I didn't need to respond with words. The heart knows. It softens the grip on the ways of seeing and knowing that we've clung to for 150 years.

It sees white birch in winter snows.

As I sit inside by the fire wintering over with the dying crab apple tree, I wonder about the original stories, the original words of my ancestors. I suspect that if I knew them, and if all the teachers in this land knew theirs, we would no longer want to teach dominion and distance.

Potato

I'M NOT SURE KATIE WAS IN LINE THE DAY IN 1847 when Stoney was overseeing the soup kitchen in Dolla, a small town near the Hughes cottage up the mountain in Knockahopple, North Tipperary. By then the potato famine was rampant and the British government was relying on wealthy landlords like Stoney to address the hunger that had spread across the island nation. My eleven-year-old great-great-grandmother Katie would have been hungry. Very hungry.

In Katie's day, Cups and Lumpers were the favored type of potato. Other popular potatoes grown by Irish farmers included Bangors, Red Americans, Ash Leaf, Kidneys, English Reds, Gold Funders, Scotch Blacks, and White Eyes. Apples were the most prized potato because they kept the longest. A good potato year, no matter the type, was never guaranteed. The soil around Knockahopple is poor and wet and much more suited for grazing animals than growing crops to feed a family.

Hunger was no stranger to the farmers on the lonely Horse Hill. Katie's parents would have been teenagers when North Tipperary experienced potato failure in the 1820s. One observer noted: "The gentry are so used to seeing distress that it does not shock them; they see naked people and they are not aware that it is not the usual and proper way for them to exist."

In 1845, North Tipperary had a bumper potato crop. In the nearby market town of Nenagh, the shopkeepers and government officials planned to close the books in the black. No one would starve in the Hughes family. Mrs. Hughes could relax knowing she had plenty of potato eyes for next spring's planting. Still, every farmer knows that the earth and skies offer no guarantee. I imagine that when dusk settled over Keeper's Hat, the family said prayers for their Apples and Cups around the hearth of their mountainside cottage.

"For some days we have had a considerable fall of rain," reported the *Nenagh Guardian* on August 2, 1845. "Wednesday night it came down in torrents; on Thursday exceedingly heavy showers followed by loud thunder peals and vivid flashes of lightning." The same rain blanketed the surrounding hills where Katie and her family would have huddled inside their cottage waiting to harvest their potato crop. The rain did not let up.

By October, the paper reported that an "awful plague had appeared in the neighborhood of Nenagh." Articles described the "blackish appearance" on the green potato mounds growing in and around Nenagh. Farmers, like the Hughes family, set out to their modest fields and began digging up their livelihood, the potatoes. They cut off the diseased parts of those vegetables infected in the hopes of saving the rest of the potatoes. But by the end of November, one-third of all the potatoes around Nenagh were black and diseased. English Reds and Gold Funders seemed clean, but Lumpers, Whites, and the favorite Cups were badly affected by the blight. The

Hughes farmers and others around Nenagh left two-thirds of their potato crops in the ground, digging up and harvesting instead only every third ridge. When the Hughes family brought potatoes inside to store for the winter ahead, the potatoes began to rot just as quickly as they had in the ground.

Families like Katie's ate the few potatoes that were good and supplemented their diet with barley, oats, and turnips, though when these ran out, they had to rely on something they had very little of to buy food down in Dolla or five miles farther down the hill in Nenagh—British shillings and pence. As their potatoes dwindled, farmers asked, "How can we sow our land, when we have neither seed nor the money to purchase it?" The next spring, families like the Hugheses planted what little seed potatoes they had left. In 1846, the total amount of potatoes grown in North Tipperary was only 10 percent of the usual crop. Once again, families had too few potatoes either to save for seed or to eat until the next harvest.

Inside the four walls of their small cottage, a dozen people depended on the meager harvest. My great-great-grandmother Katie was the third of seven children born to my great-great-great-grandparents. Joining them were her father's parents. Rounding out the cottage inhabitants was a farm laborer named Ryan, and when they were lucky enough to have them, the family pigs. Records from the late 1800s show that the Hughes family owned eighteen acres of land. Owned is of course a relative term. They were leaseholders on eighteen acres of land owned by the landlord, Lord Dunnally. Lord Dunnally wasn't always their landlord and that wasn't always his name. Nor were the hills around Dolla and Knockahopple always his home. Lord Dunnally held this land thanks to a fellow Englishman named Oliver Cromwell.

In the mid-1600s, Oliver Cromwell, born and raised not far from Plymouth in southern England, waged a bloody and successful war against Ireland. He rewarded his officers with free land in the colony. Among them was Henry Prittie, a major in Cromwell's army. Prittie received 3,600 acres of Irish land as payment for his service to the Crown of England. This 3,600 acreage included the Hughes family land in Knockahopple. Overnight, the Hughes family became tenants of an English foreigner. Along with this loss of land came many other similar strategies of conquest that Katie would see played out in The Maples.

The Catholic religion was outlawed. The druidic legal system that had originated in the native Irish woods was abrogated. The educational system was destroyed. The Irish language was put out of commission. Irish were no longer allowed to hold office or run the government in their land. But the Irish resisted. They kept their religion alive by meeting at outdoor mass rocks. They told children their ancient stories at hedge schools like the one that Katie would have attended hidden up the windy mountain paths near Knockahopple.

The strength of the resistance probably led the Prittie family to change their surname to an Irish name, Dunnally, after 1689. After a major loss for Catholics that year, a group of local soldiers stormed the Prittie castle. There they held Sir Prittie hostage. After twenty-one days, the Irish Catholic farmers walked out but not before throwing Prittie's son off the top of the Prittie castle in Dolla. The son survived the fall and the Prittie

(Dunnally) dynasty held on to my ancestors' land until the 1920s, when after Irish independence the locals burned down Lord Dunnally's castle.

Before the biggest potato famine hit, Ireland had a public works system already in place. So for instance, in 1838, wealthy landowners—both Catholics and Protestants like the Hugheses' landlord Lord Dunnally donated hundreds of English pounds every year to support the poor in and around Nenagh and Dolla. With these funds, the British colonial government maintained workhouses for the poor and sponsored projects so the poor could work for food or pay.

In 1841, the government built a new workhouse east of Nenagh costing 9,964 pounds. One thousand poor entered right away, including six hundred adults and four hundred children. These were largely people who did not have any lease holdings of rented land. But by March 1847, there was little distinction between those without rented land and those with it. Nine out of ten farmers around Nenagh were on public works. The Poor Law Union handed out ten pennies per day, just enough for families to buy the cheapest food available to them. Cornmeal.

Many have heard that the Choctaw Nation sent $170 in cash to the Irish during the horrible years of the famine, but few know that Indian meal, ground corn, is the food that the Irish depended on during the worst years of hunger. With its companion the potato, corn is a food native to the Americas. Not from the Andes mountains of South America, but from the central heartland of our continent—Mexico and Guatemala, the land of the Maya. A family of six—a mother, a father, and four children—needed three stones of Indian meal to survive for a week. During the famine, one stone, or fourteen pounds, of Indian meal cost two and half shillings whereas a stone of wheat cost almost three shillings. A stone of oats cost much more—three and a half shillings. To eat for one week, a family needed ten and a half shillings to live on oats, nine shillings to live on wheat, but only seven and a half shillings to live on Indian meal. Those like the Hughes family didn't have much choice. The average laboring man only made five and a half shillings a week, when he had work. Add to that the fact that the Irish stomach had a hard time digesting cornmeal. "It swells their insides," wrote an observer.

This last challenge didn't turn families away from the Indian corn. In the summer of 1846, the Dolla Relief Committee, composed of nine Catholics and five Protestants, pooled their resources and came up with 91 British pounds of cash. The British colonial government added another 62 pounds. With this total 153 pounds, the relief committee purchased Indian meal and resold it at cost to the poor around Dolla.

That same year, the committee also began sponsoring public works projects, like the WPA bridge-building projects that the U.S. government launched during the Great Depression here in America. In 1846, the relief committee paid out four thousand pounds to workers to complete twenty-two projects, including breaking and laying stone slabs for a new road just below the Hughes cottage.

I don't know if Katie's father was one of the men who took the day job building the new road near Knockahopple, though it seems likely. He would have earned just enough to buy a few stones of Indian meal to supplement the near-empty stocks of potatoes in the cottage just above. What I do know for sure is that as hard as the potato harvests of 1845 and 1846 were, 1847 was even worse. There were little or no potatoes left in store, and the work relief jobs were running out. To reduce the number of men applying for these back-breaking jobs, the government instituted a new rule: you could get a job breaking and laying stones only if you were willing to give up your family's leased land holdings. For those who didn't give up their leased lands, the Relief Committee set up a soup kitchen in 1847. Between May and September that year, the Dolla soup kitchen fed 49 percent of the area's population at its daily soup kitchen. That means that almost two thousand people a day were dependent on the soup offered in Dolla. The others were barely scraping by on turnips and Indian meal.

I don't know if Katie stood in line in the Dolla soup kitchen on the day that Stoney called out to the hungry men, women, and children in line. "Come on then! Suck! Suck! Suck!" said this wealthy landlord. A child of just nine years, Katie would have recognized this call as the call a farmer's wife made to the pigs she was feeding.

When another boy in line heard Landlord Stoney taunting the families in line, he took off running in his bare feet to find the local priest, a Father Cornelius O'Brien. When the priest heard what Stoney had said to the hungry waiting in line, he hopped on his horse and rode quickly back to the outdoor soup kitchen. Father O'Brien pulled his horse to stop in front of Stoney, dismounted, and gave the heartless landlord a whipping with his horse whip. The police who were stationed to preside over the soup kitchen are said to have not interfered with the priest's justice.

As hard as it was to read about the land and the hunger in Knockahopple, the stories began to quench the thirst I felt for connection, for a lineage. Our family wasn't just made up of faceless Potato Famine immigrants anymore. We had names, a place, and real things happened to us there. But to reclaim our original stories, I needed to do more than just read history books, more than imagine Katie as she walked around the mountains to the hedge school, the sacred well, the ancient gravesite. I needed to go to Ireland, back to the Horse Hill where Katie Hughes was born.

In 2004, a few years after I received that St. Patrick's Day card from Anna and Michael Hughes in Knockahopple, my family made a visit to Tipperary. To get to the Hughes cottage, Michael, whose name is pronounced *me-hale* in the old Irish way, met us in Dolla and drove us along a narrow rutted road that veered one-quarter mile straight up into the mountain toward Keeper's Hat, the tallest of the Silvermine Mountains. Bits of straw lay about the seats, and even with the windows closed the car smelled like the countryside—sweet yet damp like a meadow a few hours after it rains. I stared out the window feeling seasick from the altitude. Soon enough, Michael veered left through a narrow iron gate and into a small courtyard where he parked the car. A dog barked in greeting and his wife Anna came out of the door to the white-washed cottage where we would have lunch.

"Welcome to Ireland," said Michael, shaking my hand to greet me formally as we walked through the low door and into the cottage. He used the word in the Irish way, which means, "You are welcome here."

We felt very welcomed. This cottage where my distant cousins Anna and Michael Hughes were hosting us was the very same cottage where my great-great-grandmother Katie Hughes was born, where a dozen of them waited out the potato famine.

I studied the room. There was an old brown metal heater, a bed that doubled as a couch angled at 90 degrees to the heater, one chair, a few cupboards with flower-painted Irish porcelain on display, a sink, and the wooden table where we all sat. The low walls were painted light salmon. There was just one window, decorated with plain white curtains. The window faced the farm entrance but was so tiny that I couldn't see anything outside from my seat at the table. This tiny porthole balanced the Sacred Heart and calendar that hung on the opposite wall. The window reminded the inhabitants of the world outside, the decorations of humble human effort. I'd traveled halfway across America and across a vast ocean, along narrow roads to these silver mountains and discovered a perfect balance between life and death. I felt safe inside this cave, this home of my great-great-grandmother. Perhaps this is what home feels like to a potato nestled deep into the earth, too. It grows deep in the earth, tucked safely in her arms.

For Katie, potato growing began each year in the early spring when her father would burn last year's crumpled stalks and spread the ash up and down the long rows to fertilize the soil. Next her mother would bring out the potato eyelets she'd saved preciously by the fire all winter long and hand them out for planting in the month of May. Everyone, even little ones like Katie and her big brother and sister, would tuck the eyelets into the little mounds of earth—this same rocky mountain earth where the boys and I lunched on our first visit to the Hughes cottage in Knockahopple. The only potatoes on Anna's table—a feast of sliced ham and tomato, breads and mayonnaise, cakes and cream, orange soda pop and black tea—were a big bowl of potato chips.

A dry, painful hope filled the hearts of the Tipperary farmers when the spring of 1848 rolled around. The meager crops of 1847 had been free of blight, and everyone who could had saved a few seed potatoes or public works' payments to purchase small amounts of seed that spring. But the blight returned again in 1848, and families went hungrier than before. One officer in Dolla, a Michael Kennedy, reported that the price of Indian meal had dropped to just less than two shillings to feed a family for a week, but that families couldn't afford even that, so they were living mainly on turnips. It was common to have "one scant meal in twenty-four hours, sometimes forty-eight hours. Food was procured by pawning and pledging the clothes of ourselves and our children—even to the last shred of bed covering in our old miserable cabins."

The workhouse in Nenagh that had been built to serve a thousand inmates in 1841 had swelled to almost three thousand by 1846 and more than ten thousand by 1850. Crowded conditions like these and the multiple years of hunger led to disease, with cholera, fever, dysentery, and typhus being the most common. Sometimes this brought the worst out in people, and sometimes it brought the best. I imagine the Hughes family members listening to a visitor huddled by the fire telling them stories of the hunger on farms around Nenagh.

Katie would have heard about a fellow named Michael McGrath who tried stealing turnips from one of his neighbors. The neighbor, a James Hogan, caught Michael McGrath and grabbed him and dragged him by the scruff of his neck to his neighbors to seek a witness for the justice he wanted to offer the turnip stealer. The neighbor pleaded with Hogan to let McGrath go, and so Hogan relented, but not without first shooting McGrath in the arm as he ran off.

Others families kept the hungry away from their doorsteps because of fear of the fever that was spreading through the mountainous cottages faster than the spring fires that started the potato planting each spring. Constable Laffan took pity on one such man, a John O'Brien, and put him to rest up in William Hardy's barn. When the constable returned that evening, he found O'Brien gnawing at a sod of turf. Though he left him with food and dry clothing for the night, when the constable returned the next morning, John O'Brien was dead.

Some of the stories Katie might have heard by the fire retained hope. In 1847, two teenage girls in Nenagh cut and sold their hair for more than two shillings, more than their laboring fathers could have earned working in the public works projects around the region for several months. Many farmers helped those less fortunate, and it made a difference. A North Tipperary farmer named Billy Hough traded "useless pieces of iron" for food. Tony Dwyer carried Indian meal in his hat to a family that was so hungry the meal was the only thing that kept them from going to bed to die. Not everyone woke up.

By some miracle, Katie and her family survived these lean times, hibernating through the long hungry years in this cave, dug below the remote, rocky Keeper's Hat. I don't know what little they ate, or if they lost sleep after guarding a small store of turnips. I do know that in the years following the famine, fever and disease took more lives than the hunger ever had. Fever took her father, my great-great-great-grandfather. For Katie—a girl and a middle child, with no chance of land or a husband—this was devastating. Without a father to protect her, young Katie joined the hundreds of thousands of Irish immigrants on their journey away from the island nation. She was only sixteen years old when she made her way out down the rutted road to Dolla, down the narrow lanes into Nenagh, following the Shannon River to Limerick, and across the Atlantic Ocean to America and into The Maples.

COMING HOME

Red Hawthorn

THE STORY OF MY FAMILY'S EXODUS BEGAN TO make sense in a new way when I was in Ireland. I walked the hill where my great-great-grandmother was born and touched the earth that held our ancestors. I saw the rocky soil where the potatoes grew rotten, the cottage where Katie's father died of fever. I could begin to feel the grief of leaving our ancient trees. Not cedars, but hawthorns. Rosy red hawthorns. I'll never forget the day I first met this magical tree.

We were getting ready to leave the Hughes cottage and head back into Michael's car and down the mountain to Dolla. United across time and place, family from two continents stood outside talking. At the front gate, a tree caught my eye. Neither very short nor very tall, it opened into a firm but fine umbrella with shiny green leaves. Red berries sparkled from its angular arms, not unlike the crab apples in my front yard back in Minnesota.

"What kind of tree is that?" I asked my cousin Anna.

She and Michael turned in the direction I was pointing. Anna answered right away. Perhaps it was her Irish accent or quick delivery, but I couldn't understand her.

It took three times before I made out the name of this showy tree.

Hawthorn.

Red hawthorn.

Though I'm told their blossoms are beautiful, the tiny red haw berry has less meat or flavor than a crab apple. Yet the hawthorn is revered in Ireland, in part for its tenacity. There's an old Irish saying: "When all else fails, there's always the haw."

Ireland used to be almost entirely covered in trees. Deforestation began about six thousand years ago when the Irish tribes transitioned from herding cows to agriculture. Conquerors from another land, however, are believed to be the greatest cause of Irish deforestation—the English. But long before the English arrived and before Irish tenants depended on the potato for survival, the Irish revered their native trees.

Ancient Irish tribes built forts in large circles around oak trees. Chiefs were inaugurated next to these central oaks. If one tribe wanted to declare war, they would sneak into their opponent's ring fort and cut down their oak. For defense, the chiefs of ancient Ireland relied on the Fenians. To become a Fenian, young men underwent rigorous training in the forests for twenty years. It is said they had to memorize twelve books of poetry, leap over a stick held at eye level, leap under a stick held only to their trainer's knee, remove a thorn in their foot while running at high speed, fight nine fellow warriors with just a shield and a hazel stick while buried to the waist in the ground. When they weren't fighting, the Fenians retreated to the woods to commune with the trees and the spirits that resided within.

The druids—the native Irish class of spiritual healers, teachers, historians, and judges—also revered
and worshipped the oaks. The name *druid* comes from
the root Irish word *dru*, a derivative of the Irish word
for oak, *adair*. When Christianity arrived, the Irish retained their earlier connections to the earth, including
their reverence for trees. Ireland's most beloved saint,
St. Brigid, established her monastery in a sacred oak
grove—at Kildare—where even today nuns keep her fire
burning.

Very few native oaks or any first-growth trees remain in Ireland. But hawthorns—like the one growing brightly at my cousin's gate in Knockahopple—still
grow everywhere. They grow in farmers' fields, in hedges, at front gates, and even at Tara Hill, the thousands-
year-old ancient gathering place for the tribes of Ireland.

Why?

Hawthorns are fairy trees. They mark the entrance
to other worlds. No one cuts them down for fear it will
bring bad luck. The ancient Irish respect for trees and all
beings, even those that cannot be seen with the naked
eye, lives on. I wasn't surprised when I learned that a
friend of a friend, both of whom are university profes-
sors in Ireland, brings a bit of whiskey to the fairies in
the hawthorn in his back yard.

After the visit to Knockahopple, I carried the memory of the red hawthorn tree home with me, a reminder
to connect with respect, not dominion. I realized what
I needed to do next. Time to put away the books and
walk the land and the trees in The Maples as well.

In the early years of this journey, at least a decade before the breakdown on I-94 or before that first visit to Ireland, I had traveled by car up the interstate to The Maples. Though the town has been renamed St. Wendel, the route hasn't changed. The modern highway overlays an oxcart trail that Katie Hughes and John Meagher would have taken to The Maples in 1858. The oxcart trail follows an even older Indian trail. Yet it couldn't have been an easy journey. After leaving her whole world behind her, a world that wrapped around the hills of Knockahopple and Dolla, Katie was entering into lands and woods whose names and songs she did not know. Did her sorrow and fear echo in these leafy hills?

My first trip to the old Hughes homestead was easy by comparison. I followed two maps given to me by a librarian at the Stearns History Museum: an 1896 plat map of The Maples Township and a modern-day highway map. The older map was faded, but brown pen ink clearly showed the Meagher homestead labeled in Section 18. On the modern map a road bisects Section 18, right through the old Meagher homestead. Highway 3.

When I reached the town of St. Joseph, I turned onto Highway 3 at the south fork of the Watab River, the boundary line that had divided the Dakota and Ojibwe in the 1825 treaty. Orange columbine bloomed along the banks on my first visit. When I reached a tamarack bog—like the one I'd read about the Meaghers traversing to baptize one of their daughters in St. Joseph before they had their own church in The Maples—I slowed down.

Section 18 was just past the bog, owned now by people my family didn't know. The sugar maples were gone. I pulled over to the shoulder of the road. When

I squinted through a hedge of bushes, I made out a modern ranch home. At one edge of the property sat a second-growth shelterbelt. Directly across the road stood some trees and cornfields that formed a green blanket stretching into the winds. I remember wanting to feel a connection to this place, this square, but I didn't.

Was that because my family had broken the unwritten Irish law and cut down the trees? Or because I hadn't yet pieced together the true story of the land the Meaghers had taken from our Native hosts?

At the history museum in St. Cloud I had discovered a photograph of seven men who felled the trees in The Maples. It's likely my great-great-grandfather was among them. The men wore dark overalls, long-sleeved white shirts, and an assortment of hats ranging from cowboy hats to plaid woolen caps. Even though there was snow on the ground, the lumberjacks weren't wearing any jackets. In front of them a thick blanket of logs spread horizontally across the ground. Behind them stood a row of upright tree trunks. The treetops were too high to fit into the frame.

Turns out these Paul Bunyans hadn't cut down all the maples.

In the late 2000s, I learned of a biologist in St. Cloud, Max Partch, who in the 1950s had purchased and saved eighty acres adjacent to Section 18 in The Maples. This tract contained a stand of first-growth maples that had miraculously escaped logging. For the next thirty years, Max chronicled the trees and plants. As a graduate student, he had studied under the famous American environmentalist Aldo Leopold. Maples were Max's Sand County, his Walden Pond. Before he died, Max made provisions to preserve his woods. Today, they are a state-designated Scientific and Natural Area (SNA) and one of the only virgin maple stands left in Minnesota.

After our visit to Ireland, I wanted to return to The Maples and find Max Partch's trees. What would the stand of virgin maples have to say about the lineage of pain cupped in my hands? About Katie who left one hungry hill only to cause Native families harm? I didn't have success finding the Partch SNA until a few years ago, when I met a kind nun from St. Benedict's Monastery in St. Joseph while working on a writing project there. Hers was the same order that ran three Indian boarding schools in Minnesota. When she learned about my quest, she wanted to help.

We set a time to drive the ten miles from St. Ben's to The Maples to find the Partch woods. The nun sat in the passenger seat, holding several maps I'd collected over the years. Then we headed out, driving through the town of St. Joseph and crossing onto Highway 3 past the Watab River. From there we made our way back through the rolling hills, past small working farms and suburban ranch houses. When we reached the town of The Maples, we realized we had gone too far, missing both the old homestead and Max's preserved woods.

"No matter," consoled the nun. "Let's have a look in town." I turned right into The Maples where an abandoned dance hall, a tavern, a cemetery, a modern-day ball field, and St. Columbkille Catholic Church line the main street. This is the land of Lake Wobegon. Truly, Garrison Keillor's model for his fictional world is next door in Avon, Minnesota.

We parked first in front of St. Columbkille. This wooden, white clapboard church would have been built from the maple grove that once covered this town-land. Inside the dim relic, tall rectangular stained glass windows were dedicated to the Irish immigrants who built it back in the 1880s. When we exited the sanctuary, the nun declared, "Time for the bar."

Driving down one block, we stopped in front of a low wooden building labeled Aachman's Tavern. If the church was dim, the tavern was dark. Once our eyes adjusted, we could make out a large room that looked more like a diorama in a museum than like a pub. Along the dusty shelves, cans of old tomato paste and soup came into view. Ancient mystery novels lined another shelf. Musty cans of Grain Belt Beer stood atop a short wooden counter with red vinyl stools. Old lottery tick-ets hung on a string that crisscrossed the room.

Thinking the gloomy place was empty, we both were startled when a woman looking more like Mrs. Claus than a twenty-first-century bartender popped into view behind the counter and said hello. Her husband with a farmer's cap and long beard appeared like a timid ghost around a shelf to study us. As my friend had pre-dicted, the old-timers know exactly where the Partch woods were. In fact, they even knew of Max Partch, the long-gone professor who had bought the parcel from a logging company that hadn't quite finished the job. We thanked the couple and turned around to head back out into the fresh air. We easily followed the Aachman's Tavern directions south back down Highway 3. Across from the old Meagher homestead I parked on the side of the highway. Max's woods greeted us dressed in a fine drizzle. We made our way up and down the gulley and peeked into a small opening in the trees. There we discovered a small sign marking the SNA.

Finally!

My body hummed, excited to trace the leaf-covered path toward the virgin maple stand according to the SNA entrance sign. Grateful, I thought of all the people who had helped me reach Max's woods and this path to The Maples—the kind nun from St. Ben's who had stayed in the car while I explored the woods; the Aachman's Tavern couple; the scientists at the State and the Nature Conservancy; Max and the biologist at St. Cloud State University, who sent me Max's research chronicling the trees in these woods; the librarians at the Stearns History Museum; my grandparents, who had tried to keep pain and death at a distance; my father and the family history that recorded Katie Hughes' ancestry back in Tipperary; all of our family's ancestors; my children, who deserved a truthful lineage; my friend, who had reminded me that I was the dominant culture; and above all, my friends and colleagues in the Native community, who first taught me to see the other side of the story here in Minnesota.

White birch—I see you and your stories here in The Maples. Red hawthorn—I carry your lesson from Ireland with me, too. Respect, not dominion.

The walk through the forest overwhelmed my city sensibilities. Each tree had its own disposition. Tall trees reached high up into the trembling gray sky. Baby seedlings sprouted one or two leaf shoots. Under this motley multistoried canopy, I entered a world that would look much like it did when my great-great-grandparents first arrived. Like it did when the Dakota, Ojibwe, and Ho-Chunk came to these woods for hunting and sugaring.

On this and several return visits to the preserved maples in the area, I wanted to find traces of these previous guests. It was fanciful, but part of me pretended to be an archaeologist, searching for physical signs of my great-great-grandmother Katie from the lonely Horse Hill in Knockahopple—a calico dress, a pearl button, a butter churn? Her apron—her conqueror's costume? I wanted to find signs of my great-great-grandfather, the makeshift lumberjack, too—a woolen cap? An ax or an ox-bit? And keepsakes from my great-grandmother Mary the storyteller, the first child in our family to be born in Minnesota. Was there a quilted blanket in Max's woods? A wooden rattle? A rosary? Yet no physical reminders of their lives appeared in The Maples.

I wondered, too, if I might discover signs of the first families who had been banished from these woods. Would I find a Dakota maple sugar pail, a rusted Ojibwe copper kettle, or worn Ho-Chunk lodge poles? But no, nothing of our indigenous hosts appeared on the path.

Instead, I found trees.

I recalled the words of Flatmouth, the peace chief for the Pillager Band of Ojibwe. During 1837 treaty negotiations, he had explained the importance of the maples:

> My father, your children are willing to let you have their lands, but they wish to reserve the privilege of making sugar from the trees and getting a living from the lakes and rivers, as they have done heretofore. It is hard to give up the lands. They will remain and cannot be destroyed— you may cut down the trees and others will grow up. You know we cannot live deprived of our lakes and rivers. There is some game on the lands yet. . . . Sometimes we scrape the tree and eat the bark. The Great Spirit above made the earth and causes it to produce, which enables us to live.

As I trudged on toward the back section of the SNA where the virgin maple stand was supposed to be, my excitement began to wane. Deeper into the woods, the trail narrowed. The densely covered autumn path seemed harder to follow. The longer I walked, the more humid the air grew. When I stopped to catch my breath, no-see-ums swarmed me, making me cough. I discovered a tick burrowing into my leg. Was Flatmouth's ghost watching me? Did the trees know that I was a daughter of those who had pushed the Dakota, the Ojibwe, and the Ho-Chunk out of The Maples, forbidding them from living with this land as they had heretofore?

Eventually I gave up trying so hard to find the old-growth grove or relics of the past. I resigned myself to the bugs, to the humidity, even to being a bit lost and discouraged.

I opened to the woods and its beauty.

I marveled at the carol of hidden birds, some who sang short, fast, high songs and others who sounded low, long notes. I shivered as I passed a swamp filled with tanned reeds moving to the rhythm of the fall wind. The splendid-colored leaves on the path began to dance. And as if the land itself were now singing through me in three dimensions, I found myself climbing up and down the trail without effort.

When a surge of wind rippling through the trees rushed at me from behind, I stopped.

The forest grew quiet. A bright yet gentle green light filled the air. I turned around in a circle. I could only see tree trunks. I tilted my head back to see the tops of the trees.

Maples—tall, tall sugar maples.

These same trees had witnessed all our stories. Nothing was hidden from their view. Everyone who had walked these woods was here after all. Not physically of course, but these maples didn't exile anyone from the woods. The maples mirrored all our stories. The stories of Dakota families, like Charles Eastman who'd gathered sugar in woods like these as a child. Flatmouth and his Ojibwe Band scraping bark in lean times. Ho-Chunk families grieving their homelands to the east. Men who played dual roles of trader and government official like Henry Rice sneaking through the forest to treaty negotiations they controlled. Nuns and priests who traveled the woods to convert Native families and take children from their mothers. My Irish ancestors who felled the maples next door to build a log cabin and plant wheat. The German community who brewed beer and served it up at local watering holes. Twentieth-century loggers eager for virgins. Max Partch and his research assistants counting trees. Families today who commute to office jobs in St. Cloud. All the animals and plants in the understory who'd flourished alongside the trees and the people in The Maples.

In that moment—in the soft yet brilliant light of the maples that witnessed all the joy and all the pain—something inside me began to shift.

When I started working at the Indian Center all those years ago, I had felt an unnamed fear. This was the fear of suspecting, yet denying, that this nation, my family, and I prosper off stolen land. As I uncovered the true but missing stories of how this land was stolen, this fear moved front and center. I had to touch it. Acknowledge the suffering my family had contributed to. I began to name the ways the land in The Maples came to me and my family, our Doctrine of Discovery. I named the devastating hunger that resulted from separation from the land, a hunger my family knew all too well but were willing to pass along to our indigenous hosts. I named the continued attacks on families, culture, and the language through boarding schools and twentieth-century educational policy. I named my collusion in the conquest.

As my awareness grew over the years, the fear began to recede. Ease accompanied understanding and acknowledgment. However, underneath the fear, I discovered hidden layers of shame and grief. I shuddered when I reflected on all the pain Native families had experienced, and still experience, here in their homeland. How could my family have caused such harm? How can I live on stolen land? Raise my sons to be ethical citizens in a corrupt state? How can those of us who have benefited from the suffering and deception dare to call this land our home?

As I stood among the half-covered autumn branches, the maple woods offered powerful medicine for my grief and shame. This medicine wasn't physical. It seemed made of an intangible intelligence I'd not experienced before. It didn't speak in words or with citations and bibliographies. Alone in Max's woods, within the circle of old-growth maples that had witnessed all our stories, the woods accepted my story, my family's story, and even too all my fears, grief, and shame.

In letting go of the need to hide or deny suffering, the trees radiated compassion. The bright yet gentle light of the forest filled me with a warmth of well-being. I understood what the poet Rainer Maria Rilke meant when he wrote, "If we surrendered to earth's intelligence, we could rise up rooted, like trees."

When I returned home to St. Paul, Max Partch offered another gift.

I wanted to reread his research to better understand these powerful trees. Had I missed anything that this biologist, this student of Aldo Leopold, had catalogued? I pulled Max's report from inside the white manila envelope sent to me by the professor at St. Cloud State. The photocopied pages revealed the uneven lettering of words written on an old manual typewriter. There were no fancy PowerPoint graphics or fonts. Only simple tables with columns filled in with inky X's.

Still, I could clearly discern the facts from this forty-year chronicle of the trees in The Maples. Sugar maples, of course, had always been the most plentiful tree in the preserve. But in their company were fifteen other kinds of trees: black maple, red maple, ironwood, basswood, elm, red oak, white oak, burr oak, green ash, blue beech, box elder, white birch, yellow birch, hackberry, black cherry. And one more that I hadn't noticed before.

Hawthorn.

The magical red hawthorn from Knockahopple lived here, too? On both sides of the Atlantic—in the hills of Tipperary and the woods of Minnesota—the trees remind us to acknowledge the past and step with courage in the present. When we stay connected to our lineage and to one another, the earth will always welcome us home.

The Chokecherry

"WHEN YOU FIND THE TRUTH, WHAT ARE YOU going to do with it?"

I almost choked on my sandwich when Chris Leith, a Dakota elder and spiritual leader, asked me this question over supper a few years before he passed away. By this time, I had already completed the research uncovering my family's deceitful Doctrine of Discovery in The Maples. I had visited Knockahopple and the hills of Tipperary where my great-great-grandmother Katie was born. I had been back to the woods in The Maples and felt their generous acceptance.

Through research, I could name who conquered the land in Minnesota and whose land they had taken. The conquerors include officials like Henry Rice, who swindled tribes through unethical business dealings, and Alexander Ramsey, who led a fight to exterminate the Dakota. They included missionaries like letter writer Father Pierz and his fellow Benedictine monks and nuns who had tried converting the Ojibwe or forced them to stop speaking their native tongue. I also knew that the conquerors include, even if indirectly, all of us who continue to live here on stolen land. Across six generations in my family alone, not one of us has handed it back. This was the fear that confronted me when I had to dare myself to go into the Minneapolis American Indian Center all those years ago.

Deep down, I knew the truth. Once I found it, I had to acknowledge and address the difficult feelings that surfaced—the fear, the shame, and the grief.

Still, Chris's pointed question demanded next steps. What *was* I going to do?

That supper with Chris wasn't my first time meeting this revered leader. I used to travel down to his home on the Prairie Island Dakota Community to support a friend who did ceremony with Chris. He lived in a double-wide mobile home on a huge lot. In the open space to the east of his house stood an abandoned out-building, a grove of trees, and a sweat lodge with a fire pit. There he conducted ceremonies until his death in 2011.

One night I sat with Chris in his side yard near the fire blazing inside a ring of small rocks. It would be my job to keep the fire going all night long while my friend remained in her nearby lodge praying. Chris was smoking a cigarette, leaning back against his metal lawn chair. As we listened to the quiet of the coming dusk, train whistles sounding from the nearby tracks punctuated the silence. He asked me where I was from and I said, "St. Paul."

To be polite, I responded without thinking, "Where are you from?" His strong, lined face did something he rarely did—he looked straight at me. Then he smiled, almost laughed. In the instant before he spoke, I understood. While my heart beat faster and heat spread across my face, he answered, "I'm from right here. Lived here all my life."

Of course, he had lived here all his life. So had his ancestors. These are Dakota homelands.

A few years later he had agreed to meet me and my friend to talk about truth telling in Minnesota over supper at Treasure Island, the casino owned by the Prairie Island Community. Chris was not smiling when he asked, "When you find the truth, what are you going to do with it?" Nothing softened the poignancy of this question as it lingered over our shared table. Not the smoky air, the flashing lights, or the waitresses weaving between the Formica-topped tables at the casino café. Amid all the chaos, Chris aimed his demand straight at me.

I did not feel strong or assured in any of my responses. Nervousness rushed through me as I began to throw out some ideas for action that came from a volunteer group of non-Native and Native Minnesotans that I facilitated.

Return lands to the Native tribes?

Host a truth-telling conference?

Change the paintings in the State Capitol depicting Native people as colonial subjects?

Remove the existing federal law forbidding Dakota people in Minnesota?

Make reparations to the tribes? To the families of students who were forced into boarding schools?

Require schools to educate all students about the largest theft of land in world history?

Create access to healthy indigenous foods?

All of the above.

But where to begin and how?

Since that conversation with Chris at the casino, I have tried some of these suggestions. I helped a Dakota elder put on a truth-telling conference. I secured a grant for Dakota Wicohan to write new curriculum on Dakota history, culture, and language for sixth graders. I donate to the Dream of Wild Health, a Native farm that creates access to indigenous foods, and to the Indian Land Tenure Foundation, a Native organization that works to return lands to tribes.

But even so, I can still come up short. Sometimes *how* we do something is as important as what we do.

In the ancient legal tradition of the Irish druids, or Brehon law, it is said that those who wound another without justification must take care of them until they heal. Sick maintenance includes making sure the one who has been harmed is hospitalized. It includes paying for the doctor and the nurses until they are well. It includes recovery in a comfortable bed and in a room with proper air and ventilation. The aggressor has to make sure the wounded isn't subjected to noisy visitors or dogs. They also have to make sure that the person they harmed has enough and proper food. If the perpetrator doesn't fulfill his duty, the Brehon law could exact a penalty.

Telling the true story *is* much-needed medicine for the raw wounds in this land and the people—both Native and non-Native.

But storytelling goes two ways.

Once those of us who are Native are finally given chances to tell their stories, those of us who are non-Native have to listen.

Plant medicine will teach you that. It can heal. But if you don't listen to the plant, it can kill you.

Take the chokecherry tree, for example, like the one in my side yard. Its fruit ripens in the summer, providing a delicious and antioxidant rich food. After removing the hard pit or stone, the fruit can be turned into sweet jams and jellies like my grandmother and her sisters used to can on the prairie. Native tribes use chokecherries to make both sweet and savory foods. Wojapi is a sweet berry compote made from chokecherries, and pemmican mixes dried chokecherries with meat. This native tree also offers a mini-pharmacy within its form. The outer bark is ground and used to get rid of colds. The inner bark is dried and added to kinnikinnick, used for prayers. The berries can be made into teas to end stomach pains and relieve digestion.

Yet not all parts of the tree can be used. Once dried and wilted, chokecherry leaves contain cyanide.

Healers have to listen to the plants.

Listening and waiting aren't easy for conquerors. We are primed to take action, to chop down the woods like Paul Bunyan.

When we don't listen—to the plants and to one another—new mistakes will be made.

I've made plenty.

One year when Patty and I were working the dance registration table at the Minneapolis Thanksgiving Celebration Pow-Wow, a young Ojibwe mom came up to Patty and said, "Some weird white lady was in the boys' changing room—it really freaked out my son."

Patty looked up at the mom with the complaint. We both recognized her. Last year at the powwow, this mom and her husband led a social dance. One hundred dancers or more followed this lead couple in a lively chain that wove all around the gym, the stands, the balcony, the snack stand, and back to the orange dance floor.

Before answering the mom, Patty sipped her Diet Coke to gain a little time. A horrible feeling hit my gut. Earlier that day I had found a private room to phone my sons. The mom didn't mean me, did she? I wouldn't do anything stupid like go into the boys' changing room. Would I?

Patty set down her drink and told the woman she'd look into it right away. But by then, both of us knew exactly who the mom was talking about. I blurted out, "Oh my god, that was me. I didn't realize. I'm really sorry."

Patty stared at me trying to decide whether to scold me or laugh at me. She did both. "That's the boys' changing room. You're not supposed to go in there."

"I'm sorry," I repeated, this time speaking directly to the mother rather than to Patty. "I thought it was an empty room. I was trying to find a quiet place to call my boys."

"It's all right," the mom told me, more with resignation than acceptance in her voice. As she and Patty continued talking about the upcoming team dance competition, I reflected. Ah, Nora, you've even invaded the boys' dressing room. Like you haven't taken enough already?

Clearly, I hadn't been really listening.

After the woman left, I turned to Patty and apologized. She said, "Well, you're probably not going to do that again, are you?"

Education and facts alone aren't enough to heal relationships.

It was one thing to experience a momentary embrace alone in Max's woods—a place where I stood in surrender with the trees and listened. But to listen well and in community would require more of me. It would require giving up my tunnel vision as a conqueror.

But how?

For me, the answer lies somewhere in learning how to bridge the gap between intellectually understanding and letting go of the sense of entitled domination I assumed. Up until I saw this gap, I thought I had learned pretty much all there was to understand about the pernicious war that haunts our land and communities. I didn't understand the importance of giving up being the "expert." Of giving up thinking the whole world was set up just for me and mine.

This was a humbling step. Here I was an educated woman with a lifelong passion for history, a passion that had brought me around the country and around the world—from the Lexington Green where the minutemen fought the first battle in the American Revolution, to Plymouth Harbor from which the Pilgrims sailed. During my long apprenticeship in the Native community, I had learned new stories about this land and its people. I had marshaled all the best of my research, writing, and critical thinking skills to find supporting evidence for the new stories I was learning. Yet I was stumped, stuck in a purgatory where I could see the truth but still couldn't listen.

What was holding me back? Why was it so hard to let go of dominion and control?

An answer arrived in a dream.

It turns out, I had to discover compassion for myself first. To do that, I had to find and touch my own deepest scars.

The dream revealed a jagged thorn of grief I had

unconsciously carried for generations. Until I acknowledged this grief, I could only listen half-heartedly. I
couldn't act with genuine compassion in community.
Instead, I remained a bit smarmy, condescending. My
actions—even with good intention—kept me separate,
distant.

In the dream a woman's voice appeared out of
nowhere.

"You've got to go back. Now," she said.

Go back? Was it my mother nudging me to wakeful-
ness? No, not my mother. I didn't recognize this woman's voice.

"Hurry, there isn't much time," she continued.
"You've got to get there right away."

I rolled over, curving my body into a ball to counter the chill in the woman's dream voice. I tried falling
back to sleep, but she continued to plead.

"Now, before it's too late and she's gone."

All of a sudden, I was on a plane heading to Ireland
for a funeral. I shivered and grew feverish from the in-
cessant buzzing and stale whirring air. After landing, I
skipped customs and car rentals. Instead, I walked right
into the front room of a small white cottage in the middle of the deep green Irish countryside. There I joined
a group of women standing in the front room. They
were crying over a body lain out on a table covered in
white cloth.

I was dressed in jeans and a sweater, while the
mourners were wearing long black dresses from centuries past. The black cloth shimmered with light that
leapt like fire. They wore lace on their heads, draped like
delicate armor. Though we didn't exchange a word, the
women seem to have expected me. Without pausing in

their keening, they motioned with their wrinkled faces for me to move to the front of their circle.

As I approached the dead woman, I didn't recognize her. Nor did I know why I was there. But something in the women's song, something about this old cottage warmed me. In the back room, I heard men talking and laughing and drinking whiskey.

We all belonged here. Even me, a stranger from a different century.

I turned and faced the woman fully. She was wearing the same long black dress and lace cap as her Irish mourners. But unlike the others, the woman on the table was silent.

I reached out and placed my hand on her heart, then her belly.

At first the black shimmering cloth of the dead woman's dress was smooth. But all of a sudden strange shapes began to form under my fingertips. The woman's belly shifted from being human to the landscape just outside this cottage door. Her middle filled with mountains and valleys and lush fields. Then just as suddenly, these disappeared and the woman's belly was completely covered in the trees of ancient Irish forests.

When I woke up, I reflected on the dream. I didn't know how long the grief for the land and trees of Ireland had lived inside my heart. I only knew it wasn't mine alone. It was a legacy, handed down generation after generation. Yet our family had long pretended we didn't grieve for the destruction within our ancient homeland. We hadn't allowed ourselves to feel sorrow in leaving home. We had left that story at the harbor in Cobh in a fever-infested cloak thrown overboard into the Atlantic, under a cobblestone in East Boston, in an alcove on a steamship on the Mississippi. By the time we reached The Maples, our grief had been secreted away. Covered up so no one could see our pitiful hearts.

We were just Potato Famine Irish, my grandfather had declared.

Set a match to it, my grandmother had said.

Denial is an ineffective tool.

No matter how many layers of deception or steely resolve we built, stonemasons layering bricks and mortar over centuries, the thorn remained trapped. In the Talmud there's a saying, "The deeper the sorrow the less tongue it hath." Our unacknowledged grief caused a hunger that could not be filled. It resided in our hearts long after our bellies were full in The Maples.

Ever since that dream, I no longer have to hide from sorrow. My heart is freed up to listen. I can feel the grief of our losses in Ireland. I can feel the pain of causing suffering to Native families in The Maples. Connection allows compassion to emerge. Without it, we choke on the truth. Stumble in action.

The Crab Apple

FINDING OUR MISSING STORIES IN THIS LAND AND back in Ireland doesn't mean this journey has ended. When you step off the path of dominion and back into the circle, there is no endpoint. No final goal. There is only an ongoing dance of change: compassion, care, and connection. So I vow to keep listening to people and trees whose stories I've not yet heard. I vow to uncover and honor new layers of fear and grief and shame that may reveal themselves in the process. Next year, who knows what mistakes I will make at the Thanksgiving Pow-Wow. That doesn't mean I should stop trying.

There's another reason we cannot give up shaking off the centuries-old legacy of dominion. The conquest continues.

The conquest reverberates in our schools and our laws. The Native half of our history is still not taught in our schools. President Lincoln's 1863 law remains in place, forbidding Dakota people to enter their homeland, Mni Sota Makoce.

It appears as images everywhere we turn.

Paul Bunyan—the man who chopped the woods with fear in his heart—is still prolific. Recently, the State of Minnesota used this lumberjack as a central image in their campaign for public-sponsored health care. A popular radio station sponsors a brightly colored mural on the side of a café in my neighborhood of Paul Bunyan standing in a forest he has chopped down.

The conquest poisons the land and our relationship to it.

Yes, we have begun to understand climate change, and a wide net of concerned citizens are working to reverse the devastation rampant in the earth. Yet there's a critical lesson we haven't yet learned. We still separate humans from the earth. We still stand precariously outside of the circle of creation.

Environmentalist pioneer Aldo Leopold wrote in *Sand County Almanac,* "There are those who can live without wild things and those who cannot." He forgot that all people are wild, too. This misconception keeps people outside of the woods. Just look at Leopold's student Max Partch and the well-meaning preservationists in Minnesota. Max turned over the tract of virgin maples to the Nature Conservancy, who turned it over to the State of Minnesota, who then designated the land as an SNA. Everyone in this chain agreed that people could go into the woods only to "observe and conduct research." No one is allowed to sugar or gather medicine in Max's woods. We are banned from Eden. But people *can* return to sugar in The Maples without causing harm. If we listen, the trees, with their intelligence, will tell us what is enough.

The conquest in this land even continues to exhale its vapors deep down into the earth where we lay our ancestors to rest. In 2010, remains were found buried underground at a dig site for a new credit union in Avon, Minnesota—Garrison Keillor's inspirational Lake

Wobegon town next door to The Maples and not far from Herb's home reservation community at Mille Lacs. When the bones appeared in the claws of the yellow bulldozers, all construction halted. State archaeologist Scott Anfinson told me in a phone interview that he went up to the dig site and was quickly able to identify the remains as more than several thousand years old. Per the Native American Graves Protection and Repatriation Act, a federal law enacted in 1990, Anfinson turned the bones over to the Minnesota Indian Affairs Council. They sent the bones for testing, first to the nearby university where Max Partch once taught and then on to Hamline University in St. Paul. There testing confirmed that these remains were so old that no tribal affiliation could be identified. They were even too old to qualify for reburial in a cemetery in South Dakota designed for unidentified Dakota remains. So the bones were brought back to Avon and the site of the new credit union. In the original site plan, the bones would have sat underneath a new garbage dumpster. The Minnesota Indian Affairs Council asked the builders to rebury the exhumed remains a few feet away from the dumpster. The ancient bones would be returned to earth under an unnamed patch of grass.

One town over, my great-great-grandmother Katie's grave lies protected in the small cemetery wedged between St. Columba's white clapboard church and the new baseball field in The Maples.

"The hoop is broken," a Dakota elder explained to me at the coffee shop near my house many years ago. This elder, Emmett Eastman, is a descendant of Seth and Charles Eastman, who had catalogued the joy of the sugar maples in Minnesota in painting and in story.

Eastman told me, "We need to come back together just like the medicine wheel shows us. Black, white, red, and yellow need to come together and mend the hoop."

It wasn't until recently, when I met Wambdi Wapaha, the former education director at Dakota Wicohan, that I began to better understand this teaching. He shared: "The Creator created all people as one, but he gave each group of people different gifts. To survive, we need each other. We need to share our gifts with one another. White people have the gift of motion and action. Red people have the gift of respect. If there is too much motion and not enough respect, the world won't survive."

If we are to end the conquest, to mend the hoop, then those of us who are used to wielding fire and taking action can use this teaching to begin to slow down.

Those of us who are non-Native can listen to our indigenous hosts—the Dakota, the Ojibwe, and the Ho-Chunk. When we listen we become open to rebuilding our relationship with this land and with one another. For instance, when Teresa Peterson, a Dakota friend of mine, read about the treaty history of my family's homestead land, she asked me, "You keep mentioning the Watab River. I wonder if that's a Dakota or Ojibwe word. Let me look it up." After all these years of doing research, I had never thought to ask that question. The next morning she texted me and said, "Give me a call if you're up." Teresa had discovered that *Watab* is short for *Watab Nipi*, which translates from Ojibwe to Spruce Root River in English. This watery boundary line—noted in English in the 1825 treaty dividing the Dakota and the Ojibwe—was more than a line. It carried its own story rooted in the spruce tree, a story and relationship between place and people that I would have missed without Teresa's insight.

Non-Native people can also become allies. We begin by educating ourselves about issues in Indian Country. We can all cross the imagined divide and walk into the Indian Center. We can visit the tribes. We can ask what help is needed. We can learn the difference between being the expert and helping out. If a request is made, we can follow through. Though mistakes will be made, we can remember to continue listening and try again.

Sometimes it is appropriate to take action as allies, like asking for change within our systems. We can refuse to let our children participate in Thanksgiving reenactments. We can ask their teachers to read *The Birchbark House,* Louise Erdrich's antidote to Laura Ingalls Wilder's *Little House* books. We can insist that our schools teach all our shared history and invite Native educators into the classroom. We can write to the government and our radio stations that feature Paul Bunyan in their advertising campaigns demanding inclusive images. We can ask the legislature to fund indigenous language revitalization for organizations doing amazing work like Dakota Wicohan so that Minnesotans have access to the words and wisdom of Kunsi Maka. If we are called to mend the hoop, we can also ask other communities experiencing suffering what support and help are welcome.

We can do the hard work of listening to our own hearts to heal trapped generational wounds that fuel dominion. We can go back to our ancient homelands and find our original stories. We can open to the pain of leaving our ancestral lands. Last, we can connect with the earth and all its gifts. We can honor the ancient cedars, the white birch, the red hawthorn.

❦❦❦

For each one of us, this journey will be different. Each has his and her own pathway back to the woods, back to our original fires. Each one of us has our own gifts to share.

For me, this has meant writing and volunteering in the Native community for twenty years. It means teaching my sons a wider lens of history than they learn at school. It means donating to Native-led groups and initiatives. It means continually digging for deeper understanding, like watching documentaries or attending American Indian art events. It means showing up at city meetings and asking that signage appear in our parks that honor Dakota homelands. It means saying something if someone demeans Native efforts to change derogatory names of sports teams. It means cofacilitating an unraveling privilege group in my faith community. It means asking organizations that serve me to broaden their leadership. It means making a conscious choice to bring awareness to each step of the day and admitting when I've made a mistake.

Sometimes it also means knowing when not to act, for the hoop can only be mended if we all take turns. Here's an example. After nearly a decade of service, Herb Sam is thinking about stepping down from his role as the chair of the Minneapolis Thanksgiving Celebration Pow-Wow. He tells me:

> Thanksgiving is the beginning of the holiday season,
> and it's a really difficult time of the year for a lot of people.
> There's a lot of depression and sorrow at this time. Through
> the powwow, we made a difference in a lot of people's lives.
> We brought joy. But now it's time for the next generation

> to take responsibility. They have a lot of good ideas and
> enthusiasm to contribute. This is how we can nurture the
> younger generation of leaders coming up, by giving them
> the opportunity to serve.

And still doing or not doing things isn't always enough. We have to show up in a good way.

I still am learning. Like taking over the boys' dressing room, I often act with too much fire. If I'm lucky, I'll recognize my mistake or get called out. Then I can apologize, redress the wrong. The feelings of shame that arise when I realize a mistake don't mean I'm an inherently bad person. Healthy shame lets me know when I've made a mistake. I'm human in this circle. Much better to try to connect than not connect at all. Kunsi Maka, Grandmother Earth, depends on it. Me, too. I also try to remember that as an Irish American person, as a conqueror, my family and I have covered up these feelings through denial and domination for generations. It is going to take a long time to unlearn the path of separation and silence.

To honor my vow to unlearn this legacy—to learn to live in connection within the circle—I decided to look again at the ground beneath my feet.

Back to the crab apple tree in my front yard.

After the winter snows had receded and summer was in full swing, my dying crab apple had fewer leaves than ever before. One day an abandoned nest lay on the brick sidewalk below her branches. The birds understood that the tree could no longer support them. They had listened to the crab.

The Ojibwe tell a story about the maple tree, *inintiag*, who sacrificed herself for the people by offering her sweet sap at the end of each winter. Even today the Ojibwe offer the maple thanks before taking her sap. The Irish, too, understood the power of the trees. They revere trees like the red hawthorn still through connection and relationship.

This crab apple tree was not just an object to be admired or ticked off on a list as Thoreau had done when he traveled to Minnesota all those years ago in search of a wild apple. Nor was she meant to be preserved like a statute—observed at a distance like the state's oldest red pine. This tree is our relative and we hers.

The crab apple had offered her life to the families and creatures who lived on this block with her for sixty or more years. She delighted generations of children, bore fruit for women of my grandmother's generation, made a home and food for sparrows and squirrels and woodpeckers and worms. We feasted on her sweet rosy petals in May and took solace in her woman form in winter, knowing that, like the light, her colors would return in the spring.

She had made all the sacrifices that one tree, one being, could offer in a single lifetime.

When her form fell to the earth, I wanted to be able to acknowledge my gratitude and sorrow. I decided to offer the tree an Irish wake like the one in my dream.

To prepare the tree for her journey, I began with a visit to Jim Anderson, the honorary chief of the Mendota Dakota Band—the keepers of *Bdote*, the Dakota name for the sacred site at the confluence of the Mississippi and Minnesota Rivers here in the Twin Cities. I wanted to ask if he would offer a blessing for the crab before I took her down. Though I knew I risked being accused of cultural appropriation, I also felt strongly that since this was Dakota homeland, it was appropriate to find some way to honor the connection between Dakota people and this tree.

Without a phone number for Jim, I had to search him out in the community. In September, I met up with him at the annual Mendota powwow. Oh, how I feared he would scold me for being New Agey and using Dakota tradition to inflate myself. But he didn't. Perhaps it is because I simply asked for help. Jim agreed immediately, saying he had never heard of a White person who wanted to honor a tree in this way. He thought it was wonderful.

A few weeks later, Jim, his wife, and their young daughter came over to the house. With my sister and me standing nearby, he blessed the crab apple. His wife offered a song. Afterwards, we all sat down for a meal and talked about how important it is to walk lightly on this earth—not separately but together, as the Dakota elders had taught. We also hatched a plan to return the wood to the Dakota, a small way of giving thanks to the original caretakers of the land in St. Paul.

I wanted to find a musician for the wake and I knew just who to ask. A few blocks away lived an Irish-born accordion player named Paddy O'Brien. I rang Paddy at home and got an easy affirmative. Then I invited a group of friends, family, and neighbors, asking each person to bring a favorite poem about trees or apples to share. In between searching cookbooks for a menu of all things apple—apple crisp, apple chicken soup, pickled crab apples, dried apple fruit, and apple cider—I crocheted a pink shawl for the crab.

When the day finally arrived, it was a clear September afternoon. The crab apple's half-broken form rose to meet the shining sun. I wrapped her in her new shawl, thinking of Katie and her daughters and their single shawl back in The Maples and of all the other unnamed women who had shivered in the woods. May we all be safe and protected, I said silently, stretching the handmade shawl around the shaggy silvery bark of this kind old lady tree.

When the guests began to arrive, I offered each a blank page to write an offering of thanks to trees they have known and loved. Soon after Paddy appeared with his accordion under his shoulder, we whisked a chair from the kitchen under the tree and gave him a seat. The guests gathered under the tree and listened as he opened the wake with a traditional set of Irish tunes. As Paddy played, each guest offered a word of thanks and tied a string onto the crab apple's shawl.

Then we rounded the house to the side yard where the chokecherry stood. She, too, was unwell and would have to come down. There we tied on our words of thanks and listened to another song from Paddy. By then he'd found a few words of his own and added that though he'd never played at a wake for a tree before, he knew that the English had cut down all the trees of Ireland to build their sailing ships and cities. I recalled my dream of Mother Ireland and all the trees I had grieved for.

Next, those who had brought poems read them aloud. My mother read one by George Cooper that she'd learn from the person I least expected to hear from on this day of the crab apple wake. Her mother. My grandmother, the old jam maker who had taught us to set a match to unwanted things, to stay away from the land:

"Come, little leaves,"
Said the wind one day,
"Come over the meadows
With me, and play;
Put on your dresses
Of red and gold;
For summer is gone,
And the days grow cold."

. . .

Dancing and flying
The little leaves went; along,
Winter had called them
And they were content.
Soon, fast asleep
In their earthly beds,
The snow laid a coverlet
Over their heads.

Somewhere underneath her outward disdain for the land, my grandmother had loved the trees after all.

Near the end of the wake, my sister read "The Wishing Tree" by the Irish poet Seamus Heaney. In it, the poet describes a dead tree rising:

. . . root and branch, to heaven,
Trailing a shower of all that had been driven

Need by need by need into its hale
Sap-wood and bark: coin and pin and nail
Came streaming from it like a comet-tail . . .

The crab apple in this conquered capital city would rise into the sky, too.

After the blessing, after the wake and apple feast, I hired two tree men to cut her down. My youngest

son and I watched as her tired but feted branches thud-
ded to the ground. The men sawed the wood into neat
logs and stacked them at the side of my garage. Unlike
the crab apples I'd once thrown away, I didn't discard
this wood. A friend and I loaded up the logs and drove
them across the river to the Mendota Dakota community. On that quiet afternoon with no one else in sight,
we stacked the wood at the entrance to the sweat lodge.
As I left the logs at the sweat by the river, I felt hopeful.
Mixed with cedar and sweet grass inside the lodge, the
crab apple may rise up as healing smoke.

.

Acknowledgments

I am indebted to so many people who shared their knowledge, wisdom, and care with me during this search for missing stories. This book wouldn't have been possible without them and their generosity. Please accept my apology for any mistakes or misunderstandings. *Wopida Tanka! Miigwetch! Pena Gigi! Go raibh maith agat! Thank you!*

I thank these generous elders and mentors with the hopes that I listened well: Sally Auger, John Eichhorn, Tyrone Guzmán, Chris Leith, Alameda Rocha, Shirlee Stone, and Wambdi Wapaha. I owe a special debt to Herb and Patty Sam, not only for their kindness over the years but also for agreeing to let me write about the Minneapolis Thanksgiving Celebration Pow-Wow.

I would like to thank the many friends and colleagues who have helped me understand our Minnesota stories, including Joe Allen and Becca Dallinger, Jewell Arcoren, Gerry Auginash, Trentt Cramer, Kirsten Delegard, Antonio Dirzo, Martin Dowling, Frances Fairbanks, Marlon Ferey, Vonda Gluck, David Hall, Lenief Heimstead, Shawnee Hunt, Dave and Valerie Larsen, Mary LeGarde, Roxana Linares, Kohl Miner, Betty Moore, Garth Osborn, Janet Oshkinowe, Murphy Parkhurst, Teresa Peterson,

Deborah Ramos, Mona Smith, JoAnne Stately, Georgina Stephens, Gabrielle Strong, Patty Thompson Thunder Hawk, Kendrick Wronski, and Sharon Pazi Zea.

I thank these experts who generously provided assistance over the years: Jim Anderson, Lisa Bellanger, Ann Marie Biermaier, Eavan Boland, Barrie Jean Borich, Denise Breton, Beth Brown, Eddie Cantwell, Bill Cook, John Decker, Jack Dench, Emmett Eastman, Judy Healy, Terry Janis, Rebecca Kugel, Julie Landsman, Chris Mato Nunpa, David Mladenoff, Kent Nerburn, Paddy O'Brien, Barbara O'Connell, Patrick O'Sullivan, James Rogers, Theresa Schumacher, Larry Sutin, Howard Vogel, Waziyatawin, Don Wedll, and Bruce White.

I thank these organizations for sharing important resources: Indian Land Tenure Foundation, the Minneapolis American Indian Center, Minnesota Department of Natural Resources, Minnesota Historical Society, Nature Conservancy, St. John's Arboretum, and History Museum.

I thank Ragdale Foundation and the Studium at St. Benedict's Monastery, special places that provided time and space to write.

I am very grateful to many writing colleagues, including Elisa Bernick, Kate Bjork, Heid Erdrich, Linda LeGarde Grover, Carolyn Holbrook, Mai Neng Moua, Bridget Murphy, Loren Niemi, Donna Trump, Diego Vázquez, and Gail Moran Wawrzyniak. Special thanks are due Patricia Kirkpatrick for helping me reach the finish line; to editor Erik Anderson for his courage; and lastly to Marcie Rendon, Diane Wilson, and my sister Cate, who encouraged me every step of the way.

I thank my extended family: Andrew and Evan Hall, Liam Hughes, Michael and Anna Hughes, Dennis

Acknowledgments

Meagher, Cate Murphy and William P. Murphy, John and Sandra Murphy, Michael Murphy, Mary Murphy Ragen, and Sarann Ryan Slattery. Finally, my gratitude to all my grandparents and ancestors on both sides of the ocean, especially Katie Hughes Meagher, who lived in both worlds.

Resources and
Further Reading

If you are interested in learning more about your relationship to the land and people of Mni Sota Makoce, here are a few resources to get you started. I've included information about Minnesota tribes; Native nonprofits doing excellent work in Minnesota today; the forty-one treaties negotiated between the U.S. government and sovereign Native nations with ties to this region; and a bibliography of print and online publications. You can use these resources to find out about tribes and Native programs active near your home, and with maps you can explore the treaty trail and Indian policies that created the basis for the cities and towns where you and your family have lived. This search isn't limited to Minnesota; the Kappler online repository of treaties covers the entire United States.

Reconnecting with this land requires understanding who we are and where we have come from. In the bibliography I included many books I consulted to learn about my Irish heritage, and I encourage you to investigate the story of your ancestral heritage, too.

Keep looking and learning. The heart, the land, and all beings always have more to teach us if we only stop to listen.

There are eleven federally recognized sovereign tribal nations within the boundaries of Minnesota; four are Dakota nations and seven are Ojibwe nations. Mendota Mdewakanton Dakota Tribal Community is the twelfth Minnesota tribe and is currently working toward federal recognition.

Bois Forte Band of Chippewa www.boisforte.com
Fond du Lac Reservation www.fdlrez.com
Grand Portage Band of Chippewa Indians
www.grandportage.com/tribalgovernment.php
Leech Lake Band of Ojibwe www.llojibwe.com
Lower Sioux Indian Community www.lowersioux.com
Mendota Mdewakanton Dakota Tribal Community
www.mendotadakota.com/mn
Mille Lacs Band of Ojibwe www.millelacsband.com
Prairie Island Indian Community www.prairieisland.org
Red Lake Band of Chippewa Indians
www.redlakenation.org
Shakopee Mdewakanton Sioux (Dakota) Community
www.shakopeedakota.org
Upper Sioux Community
www.uppersiouxcommunity-nsn.gov
White Earth Nation www.whiteearth.com

Throughout Minnesota and all across the country, Native nonprofits are doing amazing work to promote American Indian sovereignty, education, language, arts, health and well-being, and justice. Here are a few Native organizations I'm familiar with. This list is not exhaustive; once you start asking around, you'll find other groups active in your community.

Ain Dah Yung Center www.adycenter.org
All My Relations Arts www.allmyrelationsarts.com
Birchbark Books and Wiigwaas Press
www.birchbarkbooks.com/wiigwaas-press
Dakota Wicohan www.dakotawicohan.com
Division of Indian Work www.diw-mn.org/home
Dream of Wild Health www.dreamofwildhealth.org
Indian Land Tenure Foundation www.iltf.org
Indigenous Peoples Task Force
www.indigenouspeoplestf.org
Migizi Communications www.migizi.org
Minneapolis American Indian Center www.maicnet.org
Minnesota Indian Women's Resource Center
www.miwrc.org
Montessori American Indian Childcare Center
www.americanindianmontessori.net
Nawayee Center School www.centerschool.org
New Native Theatre www.newnativetheatre.org
Raving Native Productions www.facebook.com/
Raving-Native-Productions-466636826859485
The Circle: Native American News and Arts
www.thecirclenews.org
White Earth Land Recovery Project www.welrp.org
Wicoie Nandagikendan www.wicoienandagikendan.org

A CHRONOLOGY OF TREATIES INVOLVING INDIGENOUS
PEOPLE AND LAND WITHIN MINNESOTA TERRITORY
This annotated chronology of Minnesota treaties was prepared for the exhibit "Why Treaties Matter" developed by the Minnesota Indian Affairs Council, Minnesota Humanities Center, and the Smithsonian National

Museum of the American Indian. The list is compiled from two U.S. government records: the Schedule of Indian Land Cessions, U.S. Congressional Documents and Debates, 1774–1875; and *Kappler's Indian Affairs: Laws and Treaties*, vol. II (Washington, D.C.: Government Printing Office).

1805 Sioux
Signed at Pike Island, Minnesota, September 23, 1805

1815 Sioux of the Lakes
Signed at Portage des Sioux, Missouri, July 19, 1815

1815 Sioux of St. Peters River
Signed at Portage des Sioux, Missouri, July 19, 1815

1815 Yankton Sioux
Signed at Portage des Sioux, Missouri, July 19, 1815

1816 Sioux
Signed at St. Louis, Missouri, June 1, 1816

1825 Sioux etc.
Signed at Prairie du Chien, Wisconsin, August 19, 1825

1826 Chippewa
Signed at Duluth, Minnesota, August 5, 1826

1830 Sauk Foxes etc.
Signed at Prairie du Chien, Wisconsin, July 15, 1830, and Stanley Co., South Dakota, September 4, 1830

1832 Winnebago
Signed at Rock Island, Illinois, September 15, 1832

1836 Sioux, Wabasha's Band
Place of signature not given, signed September 10, 1836

1836 Treaty with the Sioux (Wahpekute, Sisseton, Mdewakanton)
Signed at St. Peters, Minnesota, November 30, 1836

1837 Chippewa (Second)
Signed at St. Peters, Minnesota, July 29, 1837

1837 Sioux
Signed at Washington, D.C., September 29, 1837

1837 Sac Fox
Signed at Washington, D.C., October 21, 1837

1837 Sac Fox
Signed at Washington, D.C., October 21, 1837

1837 Yankton Sioux
Signed at Washington, D.C., October 21, 1837

1837 Winnebago
Signed at Washington, D.C., November 1, 1837

1846 Winnebago
Signed at Washington, D.C., October 13, 1846

1847 Chippewa of the Mississippi and Lake Superior
Signed at Duluth, Minnesota, August 2, 1847

1847 Chippewa Pillager
Signed at Leech Lake, Minnesota, August 21, 1847

1848 Menominee
Signed at Lake Poygan, Wisconsin, October 18, 1848

1851 Sioux Mdewakanton, Wahpakoota Bands
Signed at Traverse des Sioux, Minnesota, July 23, 1851

1851 Sioux Sisseton, Wahpeton Bands
Signed at Mendota, Minnesota, July 23, 1851

1854 Menominee
Signed at Wolf River, Wisconsin, May 12, 1854

1854 Chippewa
Signed at La Pointe, Wisconsin, September 30, 1854

1855 Chippewa
Signed at Washington, D.C., February 22, 1855

1855 Winnebago
Signed at Washington, D.C., February 27, 1855

1858 Yankton Sioux
Signed at Washington, D.C., April 19, 1858

1858 Sioux
Signed at Washington, D.C., June 19, 1858

1858 Sioux
Signed at Washington, D.C., June 19, 1858

1859 Winnebago
Signed at Washington, D.C., April 15, 1859

1863 Chippewa Mississippi, Pillager, Lake Winnibigoshish Bands
Signed at Washington, D.C., March 11, 1863

1863 Chippewa Red Lake, Pembina Bands
Signed at Red Lake Falls, Minnesota, October 2, 1863

1864 Chippewa Red Lake, Pembina Bands
Signed at Washington, D.C., April 12, 1864

1864 Chippewa Mississippi, Pillager, Lake Winnibigoshish Bands
Signed at Washington, D.C., May 7, 1864

1865 Winnebago

Signed at Washington, D.C., March 8, 1865

1865 Sioux Yanktonai Band

Signed at Fort Sully, Pierre, South Dakota, October 20, 1865

1865 Sioux Upper Yanktonai Band

Signed at Fort Sully, Pierre, South Dakota, October 28, 1865

1866 Chippewa Bois Forte

Signed at Washington, D.C., April 7, 1866

1867 Sioux Sisseton, Wahpeton Bands

Signed at Washington, D.C., February 19, 1867

1867 Chippewa of the Mississippi

Signed at Washington, D.C., March 19, 1867

FOR FURTHER READING

Berg, Carol. "Agents of Cultural Change—the Benedictines at White Earth." *Minnesota History* 48, no. 4 (1982).

Bilosi, Thomas. "Political and Legal Status" ("Lower 48" States). In *A Companion to the Anthropology of American Indians*, ed. Thomas Bilosi. Malden and Oxford: Blackwell Publishing, 2004.

Blegen, Theodore. *Minnesota: A History of the State*. Minneapolis: University of Minnesota Press, 1970.

Broker, Ignatia. *Night Flying Woman: An Ojibwe Narrative*. St. Paul: Borealis Books, Minnesota Historical Society, 1983.

Brown, Curt. "In the Footsteps of Little Crow" (six-part series). *Star Tribune*, August 12–17, 2012.

Canny, Nicholas P., ed. *The Origins of Empire*. Oxford History of the British Empire, vol. 1. London: Oxford University Press, 1998.

Canku, Clifford, and Michael Simon. *The Dakota Prisoner of War Letters: Dakota Kaskapi Okicize Wowapi*. St. Paul: Minnesota Historical Society Press, 2013.

Cleland, Charles E. "Preliminary Report of Ethnohistorical

Basis of the Hunting, Fishing and Gathering Rights of the Mille Lacs Chippewa." In *Fish in the Lakes, Wild Rice and Game in Abundance: Testimony on Behalf of the Mille Lacs Ojibwe Hunting and Fishing Rights*, ed. James McClurken. East Lansing: Michigan State University Press, 2000.

Cline, Duane A. "Wampanoag Dwellings." *The Pilgrims and Plymouth Colony: 1620.* http://www.rootsweb.ancestry.com/~mosmd/dwellings.htm

Coleman, Michael C. *American Indians, the Irish, and Government Schooling: A Comparative Study.* Lincoln: University of Nebraska Press, 2007.

Cooney, G., J. Feehan, E. Grogan, and C. Stillman. "Stone Axes in County Tipperary." *Tipperary Historical Journal* (1990): 197–203.

Cowan, Tom. *Fire in the Head: Shamanism and the Celtic Spirit.* New York: Harper Collins, 1993.

Cowman, Des. "The Silvermines—Sporadic Working: 1289–1874." *Tipperary Historical Journal* (1988): 96–112.

Cronon, William. *Changes in the Land.* New York: Hill and Wang, 1983.

Daily Republican (Winona), September 24, 1863.

Dakota Iapi Teunhindapi: We Cherish the Dakota Language. Morton, Minn.: Dakota Wicohan, 2013.

Donaldson, Thomas. *Public Domain: Its History, with Statistics.* Public Land Commission. Washington D.C.: U.S. Government Printing Office, 1884.

Dunn, Andrew C. "Pioneer Day Reminiscences. Interesting Early Events around St. Cloud." *St. Cloud Daily Times*, March 27, 1916: 8.

EagleWoman, Angelique Townsend. "Wintertime for the Sisseton-Wahpeton Oyate: Over One Hundred Fifty Years of Human Rights Violations by the United States and the Need for a Reconciliation Involving International Indigenous Human Rights Norms." *William Mitchell Law Review* 39, no. 2 (2013).

Eastman, Charles. *Indian Boyhood*. New York: Dover, 1971.

Evans, E. Estyn. *Irish Folk Ways*. London: Routledge and Keegan Paul, 1957. Reprint, 1998.

Gleeson, Dermot F. *The Last Lord of Ormond in Cromwellian Plantation: Prelude and Aftermath in the Countries of the Three O'Kennedies*, ed. and rev., Donal A. Murphy. Nenagh, Ireland: Relay Books, 1997.

Grace, Daniel. *The Great Famine in Nenagh Poor Law Union County Tipperary*. Nenagh, Ireland: Relay Books, 2000.

Gray, Peter. "Famine and Land in Ireland and India, 1845–1880: James Card and the Political Economy of Hunger." *Historical Journal* 49, no. 1 (2006).

Green, Miranda. *Celtic Goddesses: Warriors Virgins and Mothers*. London: British Museum Press. 1995.

Griffith, Richard. *County Tipperary: Primary Valuation of Tenements: Dolla Civil Parish: 1850*. http://www.connorsgeneology.com /tipp/TippGV.htm

Grover, Linda LeGarde. *The Indian at School*. Little Rock, Ark.: Sequoyah Research Center, 2008.

Harzallah, Mohamed Salah. "Food Supply and Economic Ideology: Indian Corn Relief during the Second Year of the Great Irish Famine (1847)." *Historian* (May 2006).

Hickerson, Harold. "The Southwestern Chippewa: An Ethnohistorical Study." *American Anthropological Association Journal* 64, no. 3 (part 2) (June 1962).

Ignatiev, Noel. *How the Irish Became White*. New York: Routledge, 1995.

Indian Land Tenure Foundation. "General Allotment Act Reviewed 115 Years Later." *Messenger* (November 2002).

Johnston, Basil. *Ojibway Heritage*. Lincoln and London: University of Nebraska Press, Bison Book Edition, 1990.

Joyce, P. W. "Treating of the Government, Military System, and Law; Religion, Learning and Art; Trades, Industries, and Commerce; Manners, Customs, and Domestic Life, of the Ancient Irish People." In *A Smaller Social History of Ancient Ireland* (1906). http://www.libraryireland.com/SocialHistory AncientIreland/Contents.php

Kane, Katie. "'Will Come Forth in Tongues and Fury': Relocating Irish Cultural Studies." *Cultural Studies* 15, no. 1 (2001).

Kappler, Charles J, ed. "Treaty with the Pillager Band of Chippewa Indians, 1847." In *Indian Affairs: Laws and Treaties. Vol. II, Treaties.* Washington, D.C.: U.S. Government Printing Office, 1904.

Keenan, Deirdre. "Stories of Migration: The Anishinaabeg and Irish Immigrants in the Great Lakes Region." *History Workshop Journal* 64 (2007).

Keillor, Garrison. *In Search of Lake Wobegan.* New York: Viking Studio, 2001.

Lawrence, Mrs. Harry. Interview. St. Paul: Minnesota Historical Society, April 27, 1965.

Leopold, Aldo. *Sand County Almanac with Notes on Conservation from Round River.* London: Oxford University Press, 1966.

Lewis, Henry Poatgieter. *Das Illustrirte Mississippithal; or, The Valley of the Mississippi Illustrated,* ed. Bertha Heilbron; trans. A. Hermina. St. Paul: Minnesota Historical Society, 1967. Digitized at NIU Libraries.

Lewis, Samuel. *A Topographical Dictionary of Ireland: Comprising the Several Counties, Cities, Boroughs, Corporate, Market, and Post Towns, Parishes, and Villages with Historical and Statistical Descriptions.* London: S. Lewis, 1837. http://www.libraryireland.com/topog/

Lurie, John. "Dakota Land and Tradition." *The Circle* 30, no. 12 (December 2009).

Marnane, Dennis G. "Land and Violence in 19th Century Tipperary." *Tipperary Historical Journal* (1998): 53–88.

Mato Nunpa, Chris. Remarks at the 15th Annual Indigenous Nations and Dakota Studies Spring Conference: Dakota People, Minnesota History, and the Sesquicentennial: 150 Years of Lies. Southwest Minnesota State University, April 2008.

Minnesota Department of Natural Resources. "Minnesota's School Trust Lands Biannual Report" (June 2009).

Minnesota Historical Society. *True North: Mapping Minnesota's History.* http://www.mnhs.org/truenorth

Minnesota Indian Affairs Council, Minnesota Humanities Center, and Smithsonian National Museum of the American Indian. "Treaties Involving Indigenous People/Land within Minnesota Territory." In *Why Treaties Matter* (exhibit). http://treatiesmatter.org/exhibit/

Mladenoff, David J., and Robert. L. Burgess. "The Pedagogical Legacy of John T. Curtis and Wisconsin Plant Ecology: 1947–1992." In *John T. Curtis: Fifty Years of Wisconsin Plant Ecology,* ed. J. S. Fralish, R. P. McIntosh, and O. L. Louicks. 1993. Madison: Wisconsin Academy Press, 1993: 145–96.

Morrissey, John. "Contours of Colonialism: Gaelic Ireland and the Early Colonial Subject." *Irish Geography* 37, no. 1 (2004): 88–102.

Murphy, Donal A. *The Two Tipperarys: The National and Local Politics— Devolution and Self-Determination: Of the Unique 1838 Division into Two Ridings, and the Aftermath.* Nenagh, Ireland: Relay Books, 1995.

Neil, E. D. "Dakota Land and Dakota Life." In *Minnesota Historical Society Collections,* vol. 3. (1853).

O'Hagan, Sean. "Ireland's Emigrants Sing Songs of Exile That Echo through the Generations." *Observer,* February 28, 2010.

Ornelas, Roxanne T. "Understanding Sacred Lands." *Great Plains Research* 17 (Fall 2007).

O'Sullivan, Patrick. Keynote speech at the 32nd Annual Midwest Regional Meeting of the American Conference for Irish Studies, St. Paul, Minnesota, October 2003.

Pierz, Father. "Documents—Father Pierz, Missionary and Colonizer—I. Father Pierz' Views on the Indian Situation and Missions." In *Acta et Dicta*, vol. VII. St. Paul: Catholic Historical Society, October 1935: 108–18.

Pluth, Edward J. "The Failed Watab Treaty of 1853." *Minnesota History* 57, no. 1 (Spring 2000).

Prentice, Ellarry. "Indian Artifacts Discussed, Displayed at Forum." *Paynesville Press*, March 26, 2008.

Prucha, Francis Paul, ed. *Documents of the United States Indian Policy*. Lincoln: University of Nebraska Press, 1975.

Reader, John. *Potato: A History of the Propitious Esculent*. New Haven and London: Yale University Press, 2008.

Rendon, Marcie. *PowWow Summer*. St. Paul: Minnesota Historical Society Press, 2014.

Rynne, Etienne. "Some Preliminary Notes on the Excavation of Dolla Church, Kilboy, Co. Tipperary." *Tipperary Historical Journal* (1988): 44–52.

Simms, J. G. "The Cromwellian Settlement of Tipperary." *Tipperary Historical Journal* (1989): 27–34.

Smith, Corinne Hosfeld. *Westward I Go Free: Tracing Thoreau's Last Journey*. Winnipeg, Manitoba, and Sheffield, Vt.: Green Frigate Books, 2012.

Steen-Adams, M., N. Langston, and D. J. Mladenoff. "Logging the Great Lakes Indian Reservations: The Case of the Bad River Band of Ojibwe." *American Indian Culture and Research Journal* 34 (2010): 41–66.

Stiffarm, Lenore, and Phil Lane Jr. "The Demography of Native North America." In *The State of Native America*, ed. Annette Jaimes. Boston: South End Press, 1999.

Taatgen, Henderikus A. "Thomas MacDonaglis 'Middle Country': The Norman & Cromwellian Plantations." *Tipperary Historical Journal* (1990): 133–48.

Takaki, Ronald. *A Different Mirror: A History of Multicultural America.* Boston: Little, Brown, 1993.

Taylor, Lawrence J. "Colonialism and Community Structure in Western Ireland." *Ethnohistory* 27, no. 2 (Spring 1980).

Thimmesh, Hilary, and David McDarvy, eds. *Letters of Reverend Franz Xavier Pierz to Ludwig-Missions Verein.* Collegeville, Minn.: Scriptorium: St. John's Liturgical Press, 1952.

Thoreau, Henry David. "Wild Apples." *Atlantic Monthly* (November 1862).

Treur, Anton, ed. *Living Our Language: Ojibwe Tales & Oral Histories—A Bilingual Anthology.* St. Paul: Minnesota Historical Society Press, 2001.

Treur, David. "If They're Lost, Who Are We?" *Washington Post,* April 8, 2008.

Toensing, Gale Courey. "Episcopal Church Repudiates Doctrine of Discovery." *Indian Country Today,* July 29, 2009.

Two Hawks, John. "The Thanksgiving Myth." *Native Circle.* http://www.nativecircle.com/mlmThanksgivingmyth.html

Untermeyer, Louis. *The Wonderful Adventures of Paul Bunyan.* New York: Heritage Press, 1945.

U.S. Department of Indian Affairs. "Superintendent D. C. Scott to Indian Agent General Major D. McKay." RG 10 Series, April 12, 1910.

Vogel, Arthur. *The Story of the Church of Saint Columbkille of Saint Wendel at Avon, Minnesota.* St. Cloud, Minn.: Milles Creative Print, 1967.

Vogel, Howard J. *Dakota Lands in the State of Minnesota: The Treaties between the Dakota Oyate and the United States (1805–1858).* Prepared for the Minnesota Truth-Telling and Justice Listening

Circle and Feast. Fort Snelling Historic Site, Minneapolis, October 3, 2009.

———. "Healing the Trauma of America's Past: Restorative Justice, Honest Patriotism, and the Legacy of Ethnic Cleansing." *Buffalo Law Review* 55, no. 3 (December 2007).

Voigt, Robert, J. *The People of St. Wendel.* St. Cloud, Minn.: Park Press, 1992.

Wakuta, Chief. Notes from the Goodhue County Historical Society, n.d.

Warren, William W. *History of the Ojibway People.* St. Paul: Minnesota Historical Society Press, 1984. Originally published in 1885.

"Watab." *Sauk Rapids Frontiersman,* May 24, 1885.

Waziyatawin. *What Does Justice Look Like? The Struggle for Liberation in Dakota Homeland.* St. Paul: Living Justice Press, 2008.

Weatherford, Jack. *Native Roots: How the Indians Enriched America.* New York: Ballantine, 1992.

Westerman, Gwen, and Bruce White. *Mni Sota Makoce: The Land of the Dakota.* St. Paul: Minnesota Historical Society Press, 2012.

White, Bruce. "Ojibwe–White Conflicts over Land and Resources on the Mille Lacs Reservation, 1855–1923." Prepared for the Mille Lacs Band of Ojibwe. February 2003.

Wild Rice White Paper. "People Protecting Manoomin: Manoomin Protecting People: A Symposium Bridging Opposing Worldview." Symposium, White Earth Reservation, August 25–27, 2009.

Wilder, Laura Ingalls. *Little House in the Big Woods.* New York: Harper, 1953.

Wilson, Diane. *Spirit Car: Journey to a Dakota Past.* St. Paul: Borealis Books, Minnesota Historical Society Press, 2006.

Wingerd, Mary. *North Country: The Making of the North Country.* Minneapolis: University of Minnesota Press, 2010.

Wub-e-ke-niew (Francis Blake Jr.). *Native American Press/Ojibwe News*, November 18, 1994.

———. "The Myths That Portray Original Residents as 'Indians.'" *Star Tribune*, December 13, 1992.

Yeats, W. B. *The Celtic Twilight*. London: A. H. Bullen, 1902.

Zinn, Howard. *A People's History of the United States: 1492–Present*. New York: Harper Collins, 1999.

Nora Murphy is a fifth-generation Irish Minnesotan. She was born and lives in Imniża Ska, near the white cliffs overlooking the confluence of the Mississippi and Minnesota Rivers in St. Paul. She has worked and volunteered in the Native community for more than twenty years and has published five previous books, including children's histories, short stories, and a memoir about women's textiles, *Knitting the Threads of Time*.